Digital Minimalism in Everyday Life

Overcome Technology Addiction, Declutter Your Mind, and Reclaim Your Freedom

any kind are declared or implied. Readers acknowledge that the author is not engaging in the rendering of legal, financial, medical or professional advice. The content within this book has been derived from various sources. Please consult a licensed professional before attempting any techniques outlined in this book.

By reading this document, the reader agrees that under no circumstances is the author responsible for any losses, direct or indirect, which are incurred as a result of the use of information contained within this document, including, but not limited to, — errors, omissions, or inaccuracies

Table of Contents

Your Free Gift 1

Introduction 5

Section 1: Defining and Understanding Concepts 9

Chapter 1: What Is Digital Minimalism? 11

What Is Minimalism Anyway? 11

Benefits of Minimalism in General 16

Digital Minimalism: Important Details 21

Essential Principles of Digital Minimalism 23

Chapter 2: The Trap of Technology Addiction 34

What is Technology Addiction? 35

The Impact of Digital Technology and How It Affects Us 47

Section 2: Digital Minimalism in Everyday Practice 53

Chapter 3: How to Do a Digital Inventory and Declutter 55

Dealing with Digital Entropy 57

How to Do a Computer Declutter 58

How to Declutter Your Files 68

Decluttering Your Phone 78

Declutter Your Internet Usage............................. 82

Decluttering Your Inbox 87

Chapter 4: The Why and How of a Digital Detox 97

Signs That You Need a Digital Detox.................. 98

Digital Detox: How to Do It 106

More Digital Detox Tips...................................... 115

Chapter 5: Digital Mindfulness 125

What Is Mindfulness?..125

Practicing Mindfulness in the Digital Age 133

Must-Know Mindfulness Exercises 143

Chapter 6: More Tips and Life Hacks to Break Free of Technology Addiction 179

Life Hack #1: Preventing Technology Addiction in Children 179

Life Hack #2: What If You Can't Get Rid of Technology Completely? Tips on Minimalist Tech Use 182

Life Hack #3: Use Art Therapy and Artistic Expression...186

Life Hack #4: Use Mandalas for Meditation 188

Life Hack #5: Learn a New Life Skill 190

Life Hack #6: Pick Up a New Skill or Talent That Keeps You Away from Digital Media/Technology 190

Life Hack #7: Use Digital Technology to Reach Out and Communicate 192

Life Hack #8: Use the Power of Grey Tones 193

Life Hack #9: Take the Time to Read a Real Physical Book 194

Life Hack #10: Go Out and See the World........196

Lifehack #11: Use Minimalist Apps for Work... 197

Lifehack #12: Life Hacks to Save Time on Office Spaces.. 200

Chapter 7: Preventing a Relapse.............. 203

Conclusion 208

Thank you! 209

Resource Page...210

Your Free Gift

As a way of saying thanks for your purchase, we want to offer you 2 free bonus E-books exclusive to the readers of this book.

Bonus #1 – *Bulletproof Confidence eBook*

To get instant access just go to:

https://theartofmastery.com/confidence/

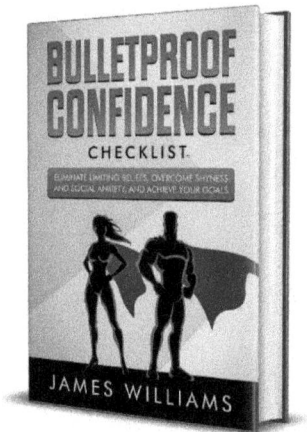

Inside the book, you will discover:

- The science and psychology of shyness & social anxiety

- Simple yet powerful strategies for overcoming social anxiety
- How to become a more confident person by developing these traits
- Traits you must DESTROY if you want to become confident
- Easy techniques you can implement TODAY to keep the conversation flowing
- Confidence checklist to ensure you're on the right path of self-development

Bonus #2 – *7 Essential Mindfulness Habits eBook*

To get instant access just go to:

https://theartofmastery.com/mindfulness

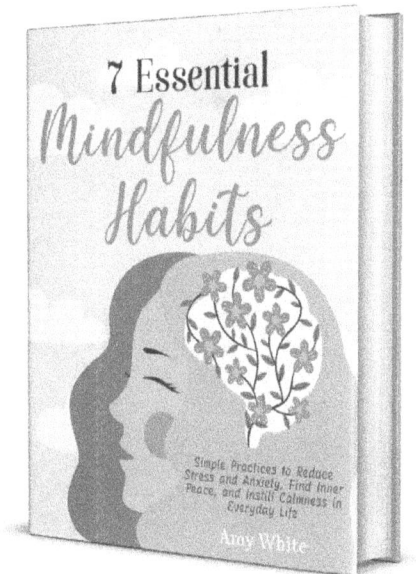

Inside the book, you will discover:

- What is mindfulness meditation
- Why mindfulness is so effective in reducing stress and increasing joy, composure, and serenity

- Various mindfulness techniques that you can do anytime, anywhere
- 7 essential mindfulness habits to implement starting today
- Tips and fun activities to teach your kids to be more mindful

Introduction

At its core, minimalism is all about getting more with less. It's more than just an aesthetic choice, but it is rather a philosophical decision. Digital minimalism is all about choosing reduced dependence on the internet, your smartphones, computers, and other devices, and regain control over your intentions, focus, and freedom to choose.

This book was inspired by lessons and ideas that I learned and practiced as Cal Newport presented them in his book *Digital Minimalism: Choosing a Focused Life in a Noisy World*.

I hope you don't mind if I chime in with him in saying that digital minimalism is indeed a philosophy that centers on technology use. I also think that we all should practice digital declutter, deprive ourselves of solitude from time to time, control our social media exposure (if not to remove it completely), and prioritize real-world experience over the synthetic associations in the digital world.

In this book, I only touch on the impact of digital media on adults and kids. I even present some numbers to prove the points that have been raised. However, I do not deal heavily with the subject of technology addiction in this book since Cal Newport has already done such a wonderful job at it. In other words, there is no need to reinvent the wheel.

What I would rather like to present in this work are actionable steps, tips, and tricks that you can do yourself so you can handle the challenges of technology addiction on your terms in your daily life.

This is a book for the average folks who can't always understand psychological and other technical terms. A lot of effort has been made to ensure that this book is jargon-free as much as possible. However, where jargon has been used in these pages, it is accompanied by explanations that can be understood by everyday folks.

This book focuses on how to live a digital minimalist lifestyle. I have also borrowed a few concepts from Newport to explain how digital media and technology affect us human beings. On the other hand, I depart from the theoretical base that he introduced, and emphasized on how you can apply digital minimalism for everyday situations.

For instance, section two of this book begins with doing a digital inventory and declutter. It is then followed up by strategies for doing a digital detox. You will also learn mindfulness techniques that will help you stay focused and present with your current situation.

Other techniques and strategies, to include going on a tech sabbatical, doing art therapy, creative work, and digital communication will be covered.

Remember that it takes time to form new habits and get rid of the old. That is why the strategies and techniques you will learn here are not one-time quick fixes. You need to spend time trying them and practicing them so they become a part of the new you.

Section 1

Defining and Understanding Concepts

Chapter 1: What Is Digital Minimalism?

Minimalism is a word that gets thrown around a lot these days. One version of this philosophy or way of life is called digital minimalism. But before we go into its "digital" aspects, we need to learn what minimalism really is.

Understanding the core concepts of a minimalist lifestyle will help you understand what digital minimalism is.

What Is Minimalism Anyway?

You may have heard people describe what a minimalist lifestyle is. Some say that it means you can only own around a hundred things and nothing more. Others would say that minimalism means that you will have to quit your career.

As you try to go over the myriad of descriptions, you might think that it's some kind of mystical or exotic way of living. The pictures of minimalist homes look really inviting.

However, living life by starting a blog, not having children, and not owning a phone sounds like way too far-fetched for ordinary folks like you and me. But here is one thing that I would like to emphasize:

A minimalist lifestyle isn't like that.

Those are not what minimalism is all about, frankly speaking. Some people might dismiss minimalism as some sort of home organization fad. Some people might even think that it is a lifestyle that is too restrictive.

Some people say they can't switch to a minimalist lifestyle because of the so-called rules and restrictions mentioned above. Just remember that being a minimalist isn't about any of those things. Sure, if you want to live with less clutter in your life, then practicing minimalism can help. But that isn't the point.

Think of minimalism as a tool.

If it is a tool, then what is it used for? You use it to find freedom. It is your gateway to freedom from worrying, fear, that feeling of being overwhelmed, consumer culture, and even depression.

Take note, however, that minimalism doesn't say that having material possessions is wrong. There is nothing inherently wrong about wanting to own a car (or two) or owning a house, or cell phones, or a shoe collection.

What you don't want is to make your possessions be the center of your universe. We sometimes give too much meaning to what we own and have, and forsake all the other equally important things such as your health, mental and emotional well-being, relationships, and personal growth.

Do you want to have a wonderful and successful career? Then go ahead, work towards your career goals. Do you want to raise kids and have a great family? Do you want to own a brand-new car and a million-dollar home?

Minimalism actually welcomes those things. However, what this philosophy or lifestyle choice does is to help you decide to own or work on those things deliberately and consciously.

If we were to summarize what a minimalist lifestyle is, here is a very simplified definition that anyone should be able to understand:

"It is a lifestyle choice where one gets rid of the excesses of life to allow you to focus on aspects of living that are equally important and contributing to freedom, fulfillment, and true happiness."

How Minimalism Has Benefited Me Personally

Speaking from experience, a minimalist lifestyle isn't easy to start, and it is one that isn't easy to maintain. But it depends on the individual—I have friends who have switched over to a minimalist lifestyle with no problems.

Personally, it has helped me to:

- Discover my purpose in life
- Get rid of the unnecessary things in my life
- Contribute to causes and things that are beyond and larger than myself
- Reduce focus on me and help me learn to help others
- Find fulfillment in life

- Grow as a person
- Focus on my mental and physical health
- Tap into my creative side
- Consume less and help preserve the environment
- Experience real freedom (no longer living the nine-to-five life)
- Pursue different passions
- Live in the moment and enjoy what I have
- Be content and not allow greed to overcome my desires
- Reclaim time for myself
- Eliminate that feeling of discontent no matter what situation I'm in

You can say that ever since I have successfully implemented a minimalist lifestyle, I was able to discover true and lasting happiness. And I hope that is what you will achieve as well.

I have long since found that lasting happiness isn't found in my possessions. I have found happiness in life itself. The good thing is that finding your happiness is a decision that is yours and yours alone to make.

Minimalism Gone Digital

You can say that digital minimalism is minimalist living in the digital age. It has become quite popular because our modern-day lives have become centered on technology. The rise of smartphones, tablets, and other personalized technology has affected us pretty much the same way as to how our possessions and other material things have done previously.

You may think that minimalists like me are just overreacting, but if you look at our personalized technology (cellphones, etc.), you may see that we have an unhealthy relationship with it.

Someone once stated that in a world where we have made interconnectivity possible across the globe, human beings have drifted more distant with one another. Artificial digital connections now replace the human connections that we used to have, and our dependence on these things has become quite addictive.

Benefits of Minimalism in General

Before we go any further, I would just like to highlight some of the benefits of minimalist living in general. After that, we will go over what digital minimalism is specifically, what its core principles are, and how it would be like in case you try out digital minimalism right now.

Remember that minimalism is a lifestyle choice that leads you to ask what specific things really bring value to your life. This is the same fundamental rule that you will follow when you practice digital minimalism. Here are the benefits that you can expect from living a minimalist lifestyle in general:

1. You save more money because you tend to spend less

When you practice minimalism in your life, you will make a conscious choice to only spend your money on things that you need. That doesn't mean you won't allow yourself some form of luxury.

You will spend money on fun and games as well, but you will be more mindful of the things you spend money on. You will learn to avoid unplanned splurges on vacations, impulsive shopping, and other financial excesses.

Since you will tend to spend less on things that you don't really need, then you will end up reducing costs.

2. Reduce stress

Living with less means you don't have to stress about a lot of things. You don't have to keep up with the Kardashians or whoever it is that people have to catch up to. In terms of digital minimalism, you don't have to stress about how many likes your post gets, how many views your videos make, and who is paying attention to your news feed, etc.

The bottom line is that you learn to be who you are regardless of who is looking at your profile or what others think or say about you online.

3. You get a clearer and cleaner feeling

When was the last time you checked the number of icons you have on your computer? Have you seen how much clutter you have on your hard drive? What pictures and movies do you have on your folders?

The first time I tried de-cluttering, the effect was very profound. For the first time in my life, I saw my house with clear open spaces. My computer desktop screen was neat, and I can see the wallpaper picture I chose.

The same thing was true of my phone. Everything was more organized. It made me feel like I'm off to a fresh start—and it definitely was a fresh start. It was a uniquely clean slate feeling, and it made me realize that I was moving forward to better times ahead.

4. A more powerful sense of freedom

The refreshing feeling you get from clear and clean spaces at home and work gives you a sense of freedom. It kind of gives you a better sense of independence. On top of that, it also influences your productivity—there is no longer any clutter that you have to pay attention to, and so you end up becoming more productive at home and work.

5. You have an opportunity to support a cause and help others

One of the first things I ever did when I started de-cluttering was to go to a local homeless shelter. I had so much stuff like clothes, food that was in storage (food that I didn't like to eat), tools and equipment, and even old gadgets that I have never used for years.

My old computer screen went to charity as well as a bunch of keyboards and other computer equipment. Last time I checked, they're using it now in one of their offices.

I packed them all up and donated them to the shelter. Helping others also helped me feel good about myself.

On top of that, since I do not throw away a lot of garbage anymore, I believe I am doing my part to help preserve the environment.

6. Focus on quality, not quantity

I have noticed that people who practice any form of minimalism tend to focus more on the quality of the things that they acquire from clothing, food, and even the apps that they download.

You are no longer instinctively lining up to buy the latest phone model or gadget. You learn to practice the principle of delayed gratification. You wait until you know that the phone you are interested in is truly something of high quality.

If it doesn't meet your expectations, then keep your old phone (or whatever gadget it may be). If your gear still performs as expected, then there is no sense throwing it away for a brand spanking new item as a replacement.

You are more mindful of your choices, and therefore you focus more on the quality of the things you purchase, whether it is software or any kind of technology.

7. More time to rest

Since you don't waste time on things, you find more time to take care of yourself and rest.

8. Invest in more meaningful things

You can spend more time and effort on making your home look just the way you want it. You're not tied to the past, and you don't worry about the future, so you can focus on more meaningful things.

Digital Minimalism: Important Details

Now that we have gone over what minimalism is, the benefits we can gain, and how it applies to our digital lives, we can dig deeper into the details. Just remember that digital minimalism is the application of minimalist philosophy and way of life in our use of technology.

One of the leading figures in the world of digital minimalism, Cal Newport, is a computer science professor from Georgetown University. He defines digital minimalism using the following terms:

> *"[it is] a philosophy that helps you question what digital communication tools (and behaviors surrounding these tools) add the most value to your life."* [1]

From Newport's definition, we see that digital minimalism doesn't only apply or refer to the digital technology that we use, but it also applies to the behaviors we have about the digital technologies that are at our disposal.

Just like physical, emotional, or psychological issues, our digital tools and products can also become an impediment to us. They make us lose our focus, worry too much, and at times cause us to overthink things. They can even stress us out or, at the opposite end of the spectrum, they can make us rely on and be addicted to technology.

In that regard, we can say that undertaking digital minimalism as a way of life can be a healthy response, especially when one is coping with potentially addictive or dependent behavior.

We do not only gauge the type of technology that we use, but we especially pay attention to the behaviors, emotions, and attitudes that we have with regard to digital technology. Practicing it means that we also need to pay attention to the tradeoffs that we make, the signs and signals of tech addiction, and our dependence on it.

Essential Principles of Digital Minimalism

When applied to our digital lives, minimalism follows some fundamental principles. Think of them as the main goals behind the practices and tips that you will read in the later chapters of this book.

People Always Come Before Technology

We live in an age when people are supposedly brought closer through the internet and social media. We are in an ever-increasingly connected world. However, despite the digital connections that have been afforded to us, we as human beings are ever more disconnected.

These technologies have rather become a force for isolation. A typical scenario pictured so many times is an entire family sitting together in a living room, but each family member has his face buried in a screen.

Where is the human interaction in that? We may be digitally connected, but it is as if we are emotionally, socially, and mindfully distant. We are, as you may call it, distracted by our screens. Our attention is sucked into the device in our hands and before our eyes that we do not realize the real relationship with the people in front of us.

So, rule number one in digital minimalism is people always come before technology. If we need to interact with someone who is in the same room, then do it the good old-fashioned way— talk.

Some people are now starting to realize that digital communication is great, but nothing can replace actual human interaction. There is something about that person-to-person interaction that we all long for, and now people realize how lacking digital communication truly is.

For instance, Antony Cauvin was featured in a BBC news report where he created what he calls a "cuddle curtain" [2] that allowed him to hug his grandmother. The video that was uploaded on Facebook leftg netizens deeply touched.

In a similar story, a ten-year-old girl by the name of Paige had a marvelous idea—she made her own "hug curtain" [3]. The curtain she made wasn't something medical or a product that was endorsed by the CDC. It was just made using Ziploc bags, a shower curtain, plastic plates, and a glue gun. Her hug curtain was affixed on their front doorway, and it allowed her to physically hug her family and get a cuddle from grandma and grandpa.

People long for that person-to-person connection. It's part of human nature. And science may have a pretty good explanation for that.

It's something called touch starvation [4]. What happens when we get a supporting, loving, and emotional touch? It doesn't have to be a hug, but that can also be quite helpful too. Sometimes we just need someone to give us a friendly pat on the back, a supporting rub on the shoulder, someone to hold our hand, or at the very least someone we can literally lean on.

Dr. Katalin Gothard, a neuroscientist, speculates that this thing that we call touch starvation is a type of withdrawal that anyone can experience. Direct person-to-person contact stimulates the release of oxytocin and opioids in the brain. Without human touch—no matter how trivial— the brain will have less endogenous opioids and oxytocin.

This is part of the reason why we adopt dogs and other pets. We all want that direct interaction with another creature. This personal contact lowers our heart rate, and it boosts our immune system.

San Diego State University professor Dr. Colter Ray explains that when we are deprived of something so basic such as direct human interaction and the accompanying friendly touch, our bodies signal to us what we are missing. Sometimes, we just look beyond the mark as it were and miss the message entirely.

We become unhappy, and at times we may even get depressed. This is because the brain is no longer releasing essential hormones like serotonin.

This first fundamental rule of digital minimalism fits in perfectly to address this basic human need—that real person-to-person connection. That is why we need to learn to emphasize that *people come before technology.*

Intentional Use of Technology

Sometimes, our use of digital technology has become a matter of habit. Okay, so what's the first thing that you do when you wake up in the morning? Does it involve reaching out for your phone to turn off the alarm? Maybe you're old-fashioned, and you still reach out to an actual alarm clock to turn it off.

What's the first thing you check when you get to the office? Do you check your emails? What is the first thing you do when you get back home from work? Do you sit on the couch and watch TV? What's the latest hit show on Netflix?

It is a fact that our use of digital technology today has become habitual. Sometimes, we may not notice, but one of the first things that we habitually do is to mindlessly reach out for our phone and check social media.

Here's a fact—digital technology today has become a force to reckon with in our lives. It is both increasingly powerful and more readily available. It is relatively cheap (depending on the type of phone you're using anyway). And on top of all of that, it is very addictive.

Today, experts use multiple terms to describe this type of experience. Sometimes, they call it internet addiction, smartphone addiction, and others. However, to make things simpler, we'll just use the blanket term *technology addiction* to refer to these phenomena.

In later chapters of this book, we will address each of these conditions and provide you with signs and symptoms so you can know how to identify if you have them. We will also offer practical and actionable tips so you can reduce the symptoms and free yourself from an over-dependency on technology.

For now, just know that one of the foundational concepts or principles of digital minimalism is that your use of technology—any form of technology—should be mindful. It must be a conscious choice and not one that is borne out of an established habit.

When we are intentional about our technology use, it is easier to break free of bad use or overuse of digital technology. We can better determine what we truly value in life and make better decisions based on those values. Eventually, our use of technology will be purposeful and intentional.

Digital Technology Is a Creative Tool

Our addiction to digital technology is based on the stimuli that we gain from it. Some people have become so dependent on their gadgets that their purpose in using them is to make themselves feel better.

You can do this little self-evaluation quickly. It won't take a minute. Ask yourself, and try to answer these questions:

1. Do you get bored whenever you're not using your phone?
2. Do you feel like you need to play games on your phone when things around you aren't that interesting?
3. Do you often find yourself checking out your social media every now and then even when you're talking to someone that's right in front of you?
4. Do you feel like your day is not complete if you don't use your phone?

If you said yes to any of these questions, then there is a chance that you may have formed some kind of dependence on digital technology. It's not just your phone, your computer, your iPad, or your tablet. It can be the same comforting feeling when you watch Netflix, your web TV, or some other device—such as any Alexa-powered device like the Amazon Echo or Echo Dot.

Here is a common response that some people may be familiar with. You feel angry, sad, anxious, tired, upset, or any sort of discomfort coming your way. The first thing you do is to find relief—and where do you get it?

You can play a game on your phone, watch a video on YouTube, chat with your friends, make a short video on TikTok, take an Instagram selfie, or maybe just check your email again even though you've checked it like a hundred times already.

But why do we do it in the first place? We use it to avoid discomfort, sadness, boredom, and uncomfortable feelings. In short, it is a quick fix. But a short quick fix is not enough.

Experts believe that if we continue to do that, we are just allowing ourselves to suffer in the long term. A quick fix is nothing more than a gate to allow us to escape momentarily. The more we do it, the harder it gets to face the actual problem head-on.

The good news is that there is an alternative.

So, what's the alternative? The other option is to realize that digital technology is a creative tool, and we should use it that way. We stop using this technology as some kind of cheap relief from pain and discomfort. We should start using our technology to create meaningful, valuable, useful, and important things.

When a minimalist lifestyle and philosophy are applied to one's digital life, you gain the same benefits from minimalism in general as they were described earlier. You will get freedom, have a lot more free space on your devices, more time for yourself, fewer worries, less stress, and more opportunities for the things that matter to you.

Key Takeaways

- Minimalism is a lifestyle choice and a philosophy that centers on having less is more
- Digital minimalism has a lot of emotional and psychological benefits—one of which is regaining control over your power to choose and reducing your reliance on digital technology

- Digital minimalism doesn't mean you will stop using your phone; what you will do instead is make purposeful and well-intentioned use of your digital devices instead of impulsive usage

Chapter 2: The Trap of Technology Addiction

Important Note*: we will be talking about a lot of behavioral addictions in this chapter, such as technology, smartphones, social media, internet addiction, and others. Please remember that there is advocacy towards classifying these behaviors as an established illness.*

*However, they are **not yet officially** recognized as a disorder or illness, according to the DSM-IV (1995) or DSM-V (2013). Note that the Diagnostic and Statistical Manual of Mental Disorders (DSM) is the authoritative guide used by psychiatrists and mental health professionals.*

We refer to them in this book as addictions because of the addictive nature of the behavior even though they are not yet officially recognized as such. We may have to wait a while before medical experts officially recognize these behaviors as actual disorders.

And now, let us continue with the discussion.

It might take a bit of effort to finally acknowledge that we are addicted to digital technology. It comes in many forms—smartphone, social media, internet, and videogame addiction, among others.

These technologies have some things in common. They were created to be used daily and they are also specifically designed to steal people's attention [5]. As they steal your awareness and attention, you become more addicted to them due to a variety of rewards programmed into the entire system.

What is Technology Addiction?

Technology addiction can be classed as a type of behavioral addiction. It might sound like a brutal description, but mental health professionals place it in the same category as other addictive behaviors such as sex and gambling.

Experts describe it as being similar to substance addiction [5a]. The big difference, of course, is that there is no substance (e.g., drugs, alcohol, tobacco, etc.) that the individual is dependent on.

It is rather characterized by an inability to limit, regulate, or control one's use of digital technology. This lack of control is also progressive, which means that as time goes on, you may lose that control further as you persist in this addictive behavior.

Some experts also observe that technology addiction has similar traits in common with other behaviors, such as obsessive-compulsive disorder.

Attention-Grabbing Equals Profit

In a lot of ways, you can say that attention-grabbing is the lifeblood of digital technology. The companies that produce them won't get any profit if their products are ineffective at maintaining your focus and attention. Tech giants like Netflix, Amazon, Facebook, and Google make use of this formula to amass sustained growth, increased revenues, and lots of success.

The evolution of digital technology and how they are used for profit has raised a lot of ethical questions. Are these businesses using technology to manipulate people? Aren't people supposed to have more control? Isn't the general public supposed to be made aware of how technology can be addictive?

Since time immemorial, human beings have been susceptible to different forms of behavioral addiction. What digital technology has done in our time, however, is to create an amplification of the above-mentioned human tendencies.

In many instances, our addiction to different things has made people miss out on many important life events. Most of these moments are things that you can never relive or have a chance to experience again.

Types of Technology Addiction

There are several types of technology addictions. They include the following:

- Addiction to online auctions
- Addiction to games of chance (e.g., online gambling)
- Footage or video consumption addiction (e.g., YouTube, Netflix, Hulu, etc.)

- Shopping addiction (e.g., buying things from eBay and Amazon)
- Social media addiction
- Gaming addiction

Many of these digital or tech addictions affect certain critical parts of our brain, specifically the brain's pleasure center. Some of these technological addictions have intense physical effects, while others have emotional and psychological effects.

Note, however, that our dependencies on these different digital technologies do not cause us any direct harm. However, as our dependence on them increases, their impact on us can be quite overpowering.

Why Is Digital Technology so Addicting?

Why is digital technology overpowering? It is very addictive.

Just like any other kind of addiction, digital addiction also appeals greatly to the pleasure center of the human brain. Since it is a type of behavioral addiction, it produces a short-term reward [5b], and it entices us to repeat the same behavior.

Every time you use (or overuse) technology, you get the equivalent of dopamine and/or a serotonin release [5c], which behavioral experts say is the same high or pleasure you get from gambling, drugs, and other things that can induce an addiction.

Note that there is an interplay of several important elements that feed technology addiction and behavioral addiction in general.

Key Elements That Feed Digital Addiction

The following are the key elements that make digital technology so addictive. And more often than not, each of these elements tends to feed off one another [6].

They are the following:

- **Distraction**

Boredom is a great need that can be filled in so many ways. The term that marketers use is to exploit something—it's not inherently a bad thing, though. What that means is to capitalize on a need to produce profits. For instance, when a band produces a new album, the producers find ways to "exploit" the new product (i.e., find ways to make a profit from it).

They would then use the material for airplay in traditional and digital radio, album sales, individual song sales, the use of the music for commercials and movies, royalties on the lyrics or the music (they're two separate things).

The same is true with boredom—you fill a need or void when you have nothing to do. People would do anything to avoid that feeling. People will do things that will entertain them, and surprisingly, people will still do things repeatedly, even if they are unpleasant.

Social media and smartphone use is a great example of this phenomenon [6a]. Some people use it as a method of distraction. Not everyone feels great after using social media. Many Facebook users say that they feel less happy after using the platform, but they still use it anyway.

Why do people still use Facebook (or any other social media) despite its negative effects? Again, people will do anything to get distracted regardless of the means. Experts say that we do it because we would do anything to get rid of boredom.

- **Variable Rewards**

Why are gambling games and games of chance so addictive? Why do people keep playing slot machines even though there is no strategy that you can apply to win whatsoever? The reason is that these games give you variable rewards, which increase the excitement that you get in anticipation of the reward [7].

The same thing is true of social media. When you post a photo, video, message, comment, event, etc., you don't know how many reactions you will get. The anticipation builds up, and the reward is finally delivered once you see how many likes, reactions, shares, and other vanity metrics you get out of that post.

The number of notifications that you get from social media also varies. Since the result is different every time, it piques your interest. You begin to think, *Okay, so how many people will like this one? Is it one of my coolest pictures? I wonder how many will react to this?*

Sometimes you have none, sometimes you have ten, and sometimes you have a hundred. One photo may have three likes, but next time you post, you may get 300+, and that will feed the anticipation and excitement that you feel. You feel satisfied when someone likes your latest video or photo update, right?

The feedback you get from social media is the reward, and that makes the behavior very enticing, which is why we keep repeating it.

The reward is variable, and it is very much like gambling. It is very alluring, and you risk very little financially speaking, but you invest a lot when it comes to psychology and your attention. In short, it is very hard to beat once you get started.

- **Vanity Metrics**

In the previous section, we mentioned the term vanity metrics. This refers to the number of likes, dislikes, and other reactions we get from our social media posts. In simple terms, digital technology feeds your vanity. Five hundred people like your outfit of the day (OOTD). Two hundred people shared your post that criticized how the government handled a particular situation.

You now have a thousand people following you—a real milestone. It's a big victory, right?

These so-called victories feed your vanity. Feeding our ego is fine; we all need that from time to time. But when it becomes persistent and gets out of control, that is when it leads to social media addiction or technology addiction.

On top of that, there are metrics (i.e., numeric and tangible measurement) that validate your vanity. Getting a lot of reactions in social media is comparable to dopamine hits.

Once you become satisfied with that experience, you tend to repeat the behavior just to re-experience the reward. In other words, you look for that dopamine hit again and again and again. This is called *dopamine-driven feedback* [8].

But it doesn't only happen on social media alone. You get the same effect in other digital technologies. You can even get the same pleasure hits when using other forms of digital media and digital technology—like unlocking your smartphone, for instance [9].

There are also vanity metrics of some sort when it comes to other types of digital media and content. We check out email inboxes, play games, ask Alexa some questions, and shop (or window shop) online out of habit just to get the same pleasurable reward no matter how big or small it may be.

- **Never-Ending Content**

Back in 2012, Netflix launched its auto-play feature. It was a binge-watching revolution, so to speak. It was the first time for any video on demand or video streaming service to provide non-stop entertainment. Needless to say, it was a big hit, and it reeled in a lot of profits.

Soon enough, other digital media content providers followed suit. YouTube adopted the same feature as well as Facebook. You can now scroll through hundreds upon hundreds of content, and it never stops.

This is one of the biggest reasons why you end up spending a minimum of 30 minutes to an hour on social media when all you ever wanted to do was to see that funny cat video your best friend posted two minutes ago. The strange thing about it all is that you get so hooked you never realize what you were doing in the first place.

Causes of Digital Addiction

There are different causes of digital or technology addiction [10]. Sometimes, the causes vary from one person to the next. Sometimes, it would take a variety of causes for a person to become dependent on certain technologies.

Here are some of the most common causes of tech addiction:

1. Depression: Sometimes, one's dependence and eventual addiction to technology can be triggered by depression. The strange thing is that our experience with our use of technology also feeds our depression, and so a cycle is made. Some people get satisfaction from their internet use and somehow forget their problems for a while. Sometimes their experience in social media can feed their depression, but they still seek out social media anyway since it is also a form of release for them.

2. The Friend and Gang Effect: Some children use gaming and social media to gain friends, and that is sometimes okay. However, when kids use digital technology too much and use it in lieu of actual interactions with real-life friends, then that eventually turns into a habit. Some kids spend hours and hours playing role-playing games online just to get stronger game characters to attract more online friends whom they have never met in real life.

3. Social Anxiety and Shyness: Some people are different when they are online. It's as if they have taken on a different personality when they're interacting with other folks online. Some people who are naturally shy or those who have social anxiety issues may turn to the internet as a way to escape their fears. Some of the shyest people can express themselves better online—as if their online avatars serve as their cover or shield.

4. Expression of Other Addictions: Sometimes, one addiction can feed into another addiction. For example, if one person tended to be a shopaholic in the past, it is possible that they can switch to internet shopping and then move on to social media addiction as another expression of their previous dependencies.

The Impact of Digital Technology and How It Affects Us

Interestingly, a lot of people don't know just how much time they spend on their digital devices. If you check out the figures, you might get alarmed at how terrible the impact of this technology is.

Researchers estimate that people, on average, check out their smartphones or mobile devices every six minutes. You can't even wait any longer to check out what's going on via the internet. We adults also check our phones an average of 150 times a day [11].

Impact on Cognitive Ability

Using smartphones also tends to reduce human cognitive capacity [12]. Ultimately, dependence on digital technology affects us just like a drug does, and it inhibits our ability to think for ourselves [13]. Experts also believe that another underlying reason why digital media and technology are so addictive is that they feed human impulses and limit our intentions [14].

Impact on Children

Note that this is the impact on us adults. The situation is much worse when our children are involved. For example, according to one report [15], the marketing of Apple was so good that 40% of US children who are under the age of nine have their own iPad.

Children in that same age group also tend to spend more time on their mobile devices. There is an 860% increase in time spent from 2011 up to 2017. They spend more time on small screens than playing with kids their own age [16]. This reduces their social skills, and playing violent videogames limits the ability to empathize with others [16a]. If you think you're overusing your phone, you better think again. Experts say that all children under 18 years old use their smartphones almost twice as much as adults [17]. This overtime, if you want to call it as such, on smartphones and other digital devices has now affected how people deal with their relationships [18]. The end result is that it has made a lot of people less happy [19]. Instead of improving connections, it has driven us into loneliness, especially in the younger generation.

Chemical Alterations and Changes to Brain Structure

Internet addiction has been found to create structural changes to the brain and also cause chemical alterations [19a]. The structural changes affect a person's ability to connect with attention, cognitive control, emotional processing, and decision-making [19b].

Studies show that parts of the brain that deal with a person's ability to pay attention (e.g., dorsolateral prefrontal cortex and orbitofrontal cortex) tend to have reduced amounts of grey matter in individuals who exhibit internet addiction.

Studies also show that the proper connection and processing between different hemispheres of the brain gets impaired when one is addicted to the internet [19c].

Experts have also found that dopamine transporter levels in the brain also decrease in a technology-addicted brain [19d]. What does that mean? As your addiction to technology progresses, the less satisfaction you get from such behavior. That means you tend to seek more of and different forms of that behavior to get the pleasure (or dopamine rush) that you are expecting.

For example, consuming the same type of internet porn won't be as appealing over time. The internet porn addict will tend to look for other types of porn to get that desired satisfaction from that type of digital media.

In the same vein, the same games won't be as appealing as before. The same social media posts won't be as funny or as entertaining. You will tend to seek out more variants just to get the good feelings you used to get.

To learn more about the impact and influence of digital technology on our children and us, I would like to invite you to read Cal Newport's book [20] entitled *Digital Minimalism: Choosing a Focused Life in a Noisy World.* It is a comprehensive work that reveals just how fraught our relationship is with today's technology.

As it was mentioned earlier, this book dwells more on actionable solutions and tips that you can do right now at home so you can reduce and eventually get rid of your dependence on digital technology.

In the next section of this book, we will go over the very strategies that you can implement for yourself at home and work.

Impact of Technology Addiction to Human Life

The following is a list of the effects of technology addiction to human life:

- Obesity
- Excessive weight loss
- Neck pain
- Poor personal hygiene
- Unhealthy nutrition
- Insomnia
- Carpal tunnel syndrome
- Headaches

- Back pain
- Boredom when performing other things besides the consumption of digital media
- Loneliness and fear
- Mood swings
- Disruption and deferment of responsibilities
- Avoiding work
- A lot of time lost
- Isolation from social circles
- Euphoria when using the internet
- Anxiety
- Guilt
- Depression

Key Takeaways

- Digital addiction affects all of us, especially our children
- It is addictive because it also taps into the pleasure centers of the brain
- Digital addiction affects us in so many ways, and it feeds our anxieties, depression, and other conditions

Section 2

Digital Minimalism in Everyday Practice

Chapter 3: How to Do a Digital Inventory and Declutter

One of the key things that you should do as you practice digital minimalism is an inventory and to declutter. Remember that digital minimalism is a process. It is not a one-time event. It's something that you will have to constantly work on.

Just like physical clutter, our digital life is also prone to entropy. Notice that when you leave things by themselves—your bookcase, your kitchen, and even your bedroom—things tend to pile up without you knowing it.

Sometimes, you forget to put a cup away before leaving for work. Maybe you forgot to put yesterday's laundry in the hamper, or you may have forgotten to organize the groceries the other day. Sometimes you even forget to prep your bed before you go to sleep and after getting up in the morning.

Don't worry. Take the time to forgive yourself for these slip-ups. They're natural, and it happens from time to time.

That is what minimalist living is for. Since you own only a few things, then the clutter won't be that much, not like how things were before. In the case of digital minimalism, things also get piled up every now and then.

That may include apps that used to be essentials for work that is now no longer required by your boss. It is also possible that you temporarily downloaded files in places where they are easy to find—like your home screen or desktop screen.

All of that is forgivable.

It's Not Just You

Don't worry; you can get over this. It's a phenomenon that is happening everywhere it seems. Here are some stats that might give you some insight:

- Since 2013, the total digital media usage in the world has increased by 40%.
- The average person today will spend at least (at least!) three hours with his face on his or her phone (or another mobile device) each day.

- For every five minutes that people spend each day, they will spend one minute of that on social media—no matter which platform.

- For every two minutes that people spend nowadays, one minute will be used for online entertainment. This includes watching videos on YouTube or other video streaming services, music, games, and other forms of online entertainment.

- The total smartphone usage in the last three years has doubled.

These trends will continue unless we do something about it.

Dealing with Digital Entropy

And because everything is subject to entropy— that phenomenon where everything just ends up going back to utter chaos—then you will have to do some decluttering and inventory every once in a while.

In this chapter, we will go over the steps on how you can do an inventory and declutter your digital life. You will have to perform this periodically on your computer, your phone, your inbox, your social media accounts, your digital files, internet usage, and others.

Let's start with the easiest place to do it.

How to Do a Computer Declutter

Your desktop computer, the one you use for work or at home, is a device that easily gets cluttered. If it's the family computer, then you should expect the clutter to accumulate rather quickly, since every family member has access to it.

Remember that the goal in a desktop declutter is to remove anything that hasn't been used from your computer in a while. This will free up some space on your hard drive and clear up the visuals on your desktop screen.

Besides, there is no reason to keep files that you no longer use anyway. It will also allow you to use your device with intention. Anything that is not adding value to your life and is just taking up space should be removed.

Here are the steps:

1. Clean up your desktop screen

This is usually the place where you can start. It is a common practice for people to download stuff and save the said downloads on the desktop. The rationale is that it is the first thing you see when you boot up your computer, thus reminding you that you downloaded your files there.

Your files are easier to find once you see them on your desktop's wallpaper. That is if it was free of clutter, right? I got started on this habit ever since I had to call Dell tech support.

I had to download a file or app to get my computer fixed, and the tech support guy told me to save the file on my desktop. And so I did.

It was relatively easy to find at first because I only had less than ten icons on my screen back then. Eventually, it became a habit, and I also forgot to delete or move pretty much everything that I downloaded.

The day I started decluttering my files, I still found that very file on my desktop after more than two years had passed. It was just sitting there, and I never really had much use for it ever since, so it didn't make sense to keep it.

Go through all the icons on your desktop—I mean everything. If it is something that you haven't used in the last six months, then delete it. If it is a picture that has some value to you, then upload it to social media or your Google drive (or some other cloud storage). Keep it there, not on your desktop.

You can choose to reduce the number of files on your desktop to only the system icons like the Recycle Bin, Network, and control panel icons. If you have apps, folders, and programs that you use frequently, then just pin them to the taskbar or dock. And then you can auto-hide the dock/taskbar so that it is out of your way.

2. Change your wallpaper

Since you're already in the process of decluttering and changing things on your active desktop, you also need to change your wallpaper.

Yes, it might sound like something trivial, but your wallpaper is something that can either have a positive or negative impact on you. If you choose a picture that inspires you to do better at work, then that should be the photo that you use for your wallpaper.

Now, your desktop wallpaper won't make or break your day—that's for sure. But it can be a source of inspiration, which is why you should make a conscious choice about the images that you will use.

If you spend a good chunk of your day in front of your computer, then using a new picture for your wallpaper every now and then can be a source of motivation to start your day.

To maximize the benefits that you can get out of your wallpaper, here are a few wallpaper ideas that you might find useful:

- **Wallpaper pictures that organize and turn your desktop into a to-do list**: Find a wallpaper picture (or make one of your own) that divides your desktop screen into different sections.
  One section would be for icons (i.e., notes, tasks, video, etc.) that you need to get done for that day. Another section would be for reminders and other stuff that you need to read. Another section can be for things that you need to do the following workday.

Choose a desktop picture that allows you to logically and efficiently organize the desktop icons you see on your screen. Remember that you will eventually add more icons on your desktop from time to time. You might as well have a way to organize every new download into a category or section on your screen.

You should also have a section for icons that you can delete immediately. If you don't need a particular download or file, then put it in that section so you can delete it any time during the day.

Here are some more ideas: you can choose workflow wallpapers, wallpapers that help you prioritize certain tasks, wallpaper organizers that will also come in handy, and to-do list wallpapers might also be your thing.

- **Calendar wallpapers:** If you're the type of person who lives and dies by your calendar, then use your wallpaper as a calendar. You can download editable calendar wallpapers. These are the ones that you can customize, like whether it should start with Monday or Sunday, highlight certain days and holidays, and a custom photo that you can choose as the background to the calendar that you will see on your screen.

I suggest using a super cleaned-up desktop when you opt for a calendar type wallpaper. That means removing as many icons as you can on your desktop or just choose the option to hide all the icons so that all you will see on your desktop screen is your calendar.

- **Inspirational quote wallpapers:** Having a quote-worthy statement on your desktop screen is like having your coach give you a much needed motivational speech. Sometimes, that quote on your screen can motivate you and make you more than willing to face the day.

  Sometimes, they can even compel you to action. Sometimes they serve as a kind of pick-me-up in the middle of the week, especially when you feel like nothing is going your way.

- **Wallpapers that calm you:** What scene brings a sense of calm to your soul?

Is it a beautiful sunset at the beach, a panoramic view of the mountains, or a photo of a local garden with lots of pretty flowers?

Any day can become an agitation— something may come up to bring you down or maybe just make you angry. To help you get over any emotional highs and lows during the day, a calming and relaxing wallpaper might just do the trick. Use colored wallpapers and choose colors that brighten up your mood. Use a desktop background that features your favorite colors.

Applying some color theory, remember that blue color gradients can be quite relaxing. If you're looking for happy, warm fuzzy feelings, then background images that have green and yellow will do well. If you're interested in colors that can give you an energy boost in the middle of the day, then get images that feature red and violet colors as a central theme.

- **Brain-stimulating abstract images:** If you need something that will mesmerize your mind, especially when the day is getting dull, then use a desktop wallpaper that has abstract patterns. Look for ones that have fractal art, psychedelic prints, or even kaleidoscope-like patterns. They don't really represent anything, but they can have a pleasing and stimulating effect on your brain.

- **Nature scenes:** Nature visuals can have a motivating and inspirational effect on the human mind. Use a picture of your next planned weekend getaway for your wallpaper.

   Your wallpaper picture can also be something seasonal—summer at the beach, rivers at springtime, beautiful falling leaves, or even snowcapped mountains. Choose nature scenes that make you feel good instantly.

- **The minimalist wallpaper:** You should have known that this was coming—yes, there are minimalist-themed wallpapers that you can download for free. They're very simple, and the aesthetics can help to drive the goal of digital minimalism home. Some minimalist wallpapers have a single image tucked away in the corner of the screen.

Sometimes, it's just a single word or maybe a motivational phrase right smack in the middle of the screen. These wallpapers help to keep the minimalist vibe going on. Plus, they help you spot the clutter you make on your wallpaper rather easily.

Choose the wallpaper that works for you. You can even change things up from time to time as needed. The important thing is that you keep your desktop clean. If you can maintain that for a few weeks, then you're off to a good start on your journey to digital minimalism.

3. Uninstall apps and programs

Just like files, photos, videos, and other stuff you download, apps and programs also tend to clutter things up on your computer. You may already have some programs that you haven't used in a while. Sometimes, your computer comes pre-installed with bloatware—apps that you don't need that come preinstalled with your computer when you bought it.

Go through your list of programs. On Windows operating systems, you need to go to your computer's Control Panel to add and remove programs. Be careful, though; you may uninstall something necessary for your computer system to function properly.

If you're not really that techie, then here's a simpler and safer way to do it. Click on your Start screen and then go through the list of apps and programs that you see there. Uninstall the ones that you don't need or use.

Remember to keep your malware cleaner, antivirus software, and productivity tools. You may have some games installed there, so just uninstall them, especially if you're not playing games on that computer. Most people play games on their phones anyway.

4. Use full-screen mode

Almost every app will allow you to work in full-screen mode. Don't split your screen using smaller windows. If you need to see multiple windows, then I suggest that you use multiple screens.

Connect another monitor to your computer so you can work in a multi-screen fashion. That way, you can have one document or file open on one screen and the other things you need for work on another screen. Working on the full screen allows you to focus and concentrate—and thus keep distractions away.

How to Declutter Your Files

After cleaning up your desktop and wallpaper, you're ready to move on to the next step: cleaning up your files. This will be a bit more difficult since you will have more items to sort out.

Here's an observation from someone who has been around computers for decades: as hard drives get bigger, the easier it is for people to accumulate junk. Back in the day, we worked with kilobyte-sized drives—you know those old floppy drives?

And then hard drives got installed on computers. They weren't much—just a few megabytes worth. And then the most you could get was around 80 gigabytes—and we were already celebrating back then.

And then the drives got bigger—around 500 megabytes (and we were still celebrating—yay!). Until today, we had terabytes worth of hard drive space. With smaller hard drives, people were more mindful of what they stored and saved on their computers.

You had very little space, so you needed to conserve what you had. And with the imminent increase in hard drive space, people no longer had to worry about storage space. Except now, you have a lot of clutter and digital junk. These unnecessary files slow down your computer system, and they bog down your productivity.

Let's go over the things that you can do to reduce the amount of digital junk on your hard drives.

1. Learn to delete the unnecessary

Remember that you can do all of these declutter steps at any time. You will also be doing them regularly, so it would be best to get started now. If you have a computer or laptop, then you can start with that. Take note of how much space you have recovered and how good your wallpaper looks.

You can then move on to your emails, your phone, and other devices. It will be a painful process for some, especially for those who have been hanging on to certain files for quite a while. However, do take note that it will be worth it in the long run.

2. Upload files to cloud storage

There will be files on your hard drive that will have a bit of sentimental value. This could be photos of your kids while they were still infants, pictures of loved ones, documents, and files that were shared to you that have some personal significance.

So, why use cloud storage?

Cloud storage allows you to store your files in a remote location that is accessible through the internet. That means you can access your files using any device that has an internet connection.

You don't have to rely on a single physical hard drive, external storage, phone, or computer to store your videos, pictures, and other files. Cloud storage improves your productivity and efficiency.

Using this type of service also saves you from the hassle of maintaining your storage device. Remember that even external backup drives also have a usable life—around five years or so.

After five years, you will need to transfer your files from one backup drive to another. But what if you forget when you should do that, and then your backup expires? One day it fails, and you can no longer access your files.

With the help of cloud storage, the service providers will maintain your data and have backups of backups, so in case one of their drives goes down the drain, they still have backups that you can use to retrieve your files.

Of course, not all cloud storage options are the same. Some are better suited for certain people's needs. Here are my recommendations according to specific needs that you may have.

- **Dropbox**: I think this is the best cloud storage option for light data users. It's great for personal use, small teams (for the free option), but they also have service plans for large businesses too. Storage options start at 2 GB, which is pretty small, but you can upgrade it. Storage plans start at $8.25, which makes it one of the most affordable options.

- **Google Drive**: This is the most affordable cloud-storage option today. It is free for the first 15 GB that you upload. However, you can choose from larger storage space plans starting at 100 GB up to unlimited data storage. Note that the 200 GB storage space plan is only $2.99 a month, which is pretty affordable. Google Drive is best suited for collaborating with your team at work or for families who want to share files with one another.

- **Microsoft OneDrive**: If you're a Microsoft Windows user, then this might be the most compatible cloud storage option for your device. They provide free storage for the first 5 GB of files you want to upload. The paid storage plan starts at 50 GB for $1.99, which makes it one of the more affordable options on this list. Note that OneDrive also works great for iOS and Android devices.

- **pCloud**: If you're looking to store really large files, then this might be the cloud storage service for you. They provide free storage for the first 10 GB of data that you upload. You pay $3.99 per month for 500 GB of storage. They also have lifetime plans where you only pay a one-time fee—no recurring monthly charges.

- **iCloud**: This may be the best storage option for iOS users—it's already integrated into your iPhone or iPad or other Apple device. It's a great option for private users—you know, if you don't want to share your files with anyone. The first 5 GB of storage is free, and the paid storage plans start at 99 cents per month for the first 50 GB you use. You can also opt for the maximum 2 TB of storage for $9.99 a month.

What you should do at this point is to decide which cloud storage solution is best for you, depending on the particular needs you may have. Before signing up for any cloud storage service, you should check out what their basic plans will give you, the allowed upload limit, and any terms and conditions as well.

3. Make your folders and files easier to search

Tell me, which of these two folder names will be easier to understand and remember:

- CB1HQ6HALH
- Work Files 2020

You will have to admit that option number one above would make a really good password, right? It's pretty random, and it will be very difficult to guess. On the other hand, option number two will be easier to decipher. The name is rather easy to recall, and it already hints at the contents of the folder.

The next step is to scan all your folders and files and rename the ones that don't make any sense, like the first option in the example above. Make the names as descriptive as you can, and make them easier to remember.

4. Reduce the number of folders

You don't need to clutter your drive with very specific folders. The search capabilities of today's operating systems have been made more efficient, thus making files easier to find. You don't have to create different folders that contain very few things.

For instance, you can group all pictures into Photos 2020 or Photos 2019 (arranging things by year). Don't worry about what time of the year each photo was taken since each photograph that you take with your device will have a timestamp and you can arrange your pictures in chronological order, which makes them easier to find.

In my case, I organize things by year, but you don't have to do that too. How you simplify your file organization is up to you. The point here is that you don't need a thousand folders on your computer. You can just use Work, Fun Stuff, and Personal Stuff to help you identify where each file should go.

5. **Shut down and give your device a clean start**

Tell me if this is one of your habits—you're done using your computer, and you just close it and go to sleep? Do you leave your computer in sleep mode? When was the last time you turned off your phone or took it off the internet?

Here's a new habit that you might want to start:

a. Close all the tabs, apps, and programs that you have running at the end of the day or before going to bed at night.

b. Move all the files that are in your Downloads folder to their designated folders. If there are files there that don't belong anywhere and won't be used anyway, then just delete them.

c. Make sure to empty the Trash/Recycle bin.

d. Finally, shut down/turn off your computer/phone

This way, you're giving yourself a fresh start each time you restart your device. If you're using your phone as an alarm clock, then just do a power cycle.

6. Don't buy your digital media—rent it as much as possible

Here's a little confession that I would like to make—I still have movies and videos that I have downloaded since the late '90s. I even have the movie *12 Monkeys* (starring Bruce Willis).

But I now have them all in a USB backup drive. I have more than a decade's worth of videos and movies stored in backup drives. Some of the ones I downloaded were movie bombs but hey, I remember the people I enjoyed watching them with back then, so it's not always about the film.

Going back to the present moment, notice that your computer or mobile device will usually have a lot of digital media in the form of eBooks, videos, documents, pdf files, and whatnot.

Here's something that I did—I stopped buying and downloading them. Unless you're downloading it for your collection, then just rent it. Let's say you fancy a new eBook on Amazon;

don't buy it if you're unsure if it's a keeper—rent it.

If it doesn't pan out, then at least you're not filling up your Kindle library with books you have never even read or ones that you have only casually read (around five or so pages). The same is true with video. Don't download videos unless you intend to watch them sometime soon.

If you're just curious about whether it's a great movie or video, then just rent it instead so it won't clutter up your device. Use the same rule for your music and other digital media. Stream it as much as possible; rent it if that option is available.

Decluttering Your Phone

At this point, you have already started decluttering your computer, your phone, Kindle, and other devices. You should have completely decluttered your laptop or computer by now.

Now, we will be moving on to something a bit more difficult—your phone. Our phones right now play a big part in our lives. Ten to 20 years ago, no one needed a smartphone, much less an iPhone. Maybe 20 or so years ago, especially when Lawrence Fishbourne and Keanu Reeves played their big roles in *The Matrix* movies, cell phones had their limelight.

Nokia was the big brand back then, and flip phones were some of the most high-tech gadgets we had. So, even before smartphones and iPhones took to the shelves, people already manifested some kind of dependence on mobile devices—they're just not as high tech as we have them today.

Fast forward into the future; we're pretty much in the same situation. We still love our mobile devices, but we only have more high-tech ones with hundreds of other features than before.

Here are the steps on how you can declutter your phone:

1. Delete apps that you never use

If you've had your phone for a while, then it is likely that you have apps and games on your mobile device that you no longer use. That can include games that you used to play, that alarm clock app (in my case, I have this fart sound app that I use to prank my friends—it's some kind of a whoopee cushion), and other apps.

2. Use the web/mobile version for apps you don't use frequently

Let's say you don't use Facebook that much. Maybe you use it just to check on your friends or maybe just pitch ideas in a group that you participate in. You don't need to install the Facebook app since you can still access Facebook using your phone's browser.

That will be one less icon on your phone's screen and one less app on your phone's storage. Go over all the apps on your phone and delete the ones that you rarely use and just settle for the mobile version through your browser.

3. Dock 'em and group 'em

Choose three or four of your most-used apps. It can be your camera, YouTube, text messaging, or maybe your dialer app. After selecting your most-used apps, you should place them in your dock at the bottom of your phone's screen.

So, what about the other apps? The other remaining apps on your phone should be grouped together and placed inside a folder. Put all your social media in one folder, your work and productivity apps in another, your games and entertainment apps in another, etc.

4. Reduce the number of social media apps

Trust me. You don't need to have some kind of presence on all social media platforms. You will still live a happy life, even if you only have a few social media apps on your device. We'll go over how to stop the dependence on social media in a later chapter of this book.

5. Clean up your list of contacts

Next, go over your contact list. Go through each of the numbers listed there, and delete the ones that you don't ever call or send messages to. Any phone number that you don't intend to call again should also be removed as well.

If you have music, videos, or even podcasts you can still find in your folders and you don't use them or need them at all, then you should delete them too.

6. Turn off or remove any notifications

Chances are your apps will have notifications. Turn them off or remove them. Delete any alarms you have set up.

7. Set up a do not disturb time

Setting up a do not disturb time, say 8 pm to 6 am, will allow you to rest for the night. That means no phone calls, messages, notifications, etc. Putting that on your schedule will allow you to focus on yourself.

Declutter Your Internet Usage

Now, here's another big step that you can take—practicing digital minimalism with regards to your internet usage. When it comes to the internet, you never know how deep the rabbit hole can be. You might end up chasing the latest trends to no end. In a later chapter of this book, we will go over how to do an information diet and a social media sabbatical.

For now, here are a few tips that you can use to reduce the clutter that you experience through your internet usage.

1. Reduce the number of tabs on your browser

Back in the day, internet browsers only had one tab. If you wanted to see more than one web page, then you had to open a new window. It was only a few years later when browsers (starting with Firefox) provided the ability to open new tabs.

It was fun at first since you can open multiple tabs and such. But then as you go along with your work, you end up with a hundred tabs on your screen. Since opening new tabs has become so easy, you don't think about it and just open more tabs even if you don't really need them anyway.

Here's what you can do—limit your use to around five tabs only. The important thing here is that you choose and know what each tab contains. Don't just open tabs because you think you will read through the page later, or maybe it may have some useful info later. If it is a pop-up or pop-under tab, then just close it; you don't need to see or read what's on that tab.

2. Monitor the number of hours you spend online

Google Chrome has an extension that you can download, called Time Tracker. You can download it from the Chrome Web Store. It helps you identify which websites you visit, and monitor how much time you spend on various websites.

This is your first step in determining where you go online and identifying your time wasters. Figure out which sites you spend a lot of time on. After that, determine which of those sites are useful and which ones give value to your life.

Let's say you find out that you spend two hours on Facebook each day, and you're old school— you're still using your browser to check out your friends' posts. Let's say that you want to stop using Chrome for Facebook.

You can block Facebook in Chrome using an extension called Block Site. It is a website blocker for Google Chrome. There are other website blockers that you can use, and there are website blockers for different browsers.

There's LeechBlock for Firefox, StayFocusd for Chrome, Cold Turkey for Windows OS users, and if you're a Mac user, you can try SelfControl to block websites.

3. Unfriend and Unfollow

Consider your newsfeed as something sacred. It's not that it is something divine or worthy of worship, but it is something that you spend precious time on. If your newsfeed is full of things that distract you, then it's time to reduce and declutter.

The rule here is that if someone, something, a group, or whatever it is on social media is no longer informative, entertaining, or interesting, and it is still showing up on your newsfeed, then it's time to unfriend and unfollow.

Anything or anyone that doesn't add value to your life right now should be taken off your list.

4. Choose only one or two social media channels

I would recommend sticking to only one social media channel unless you need another channel—maybe Facebook for work since your boss wants you to do social media marketing there.

Keep only the social media channels that you like. You have the option to delete your account on certain social media sites, or if you want, you can just deactivate your account. At least you still have the option to come back to it in case you may have to—let's say a client wants you to do some marketing on Instagram as well.

5. Clean up your bookmarks

Finally, you should pay attention to your bookmarks bar. We sometimes tend to bookmark webpages or websites at will without thinking about it. I used to have more than 15 folders in my bookmarks bar, not to mention hundreds of bookmarked pages there.

It's crazy—I have everything from movies I would like to download on Amazon to Facebook posts of my friends that I wanted to comment on later (which never happens, of course).

What happens is that we bookmark pages, and we forget about them. We hope that maybe as we go through our bookmarks, we will remember what we intended to do with them.

Unfortunately, when the day finally comes when you need to search your bookmarks, it will be very difficult to find the bookmarked page you wanted.

When you have a clean set of bookmarks, you will be forced to be mindful of the web pages that you will visit. For instance, if you want to open Wikipedia, you need to type the entire URL. That way, you will be mindful of which web pages you visit.

Decluttering Your Inbox

Studies show that average adults check their emails around 45 times each day. If you work with emails or use emails a lot in your job, then you tend to check your inbox more often than that.

Your emails aren't particularly life-changing. You will get some really important ones, but they won't be that frequent. However, you should take control of what gets into your inbox since going over hundreds of emails is a waste of your time.

Here are some very important tips that will be useful for you to clean up your inbox.

Opt Out of Mailing Lists

In my personal experience, I signed up for a lot of mailing lists from online courses to discount offers from different online retailers. At one time, my inbox had more than 5,000 emails—not kidding.

I spent a lot of time opting out of mailing lists, and then I spent even more time deleting emails. I had to be systematic about it. For instance, I once signed up for an email course about stock market trading. It was fun for a while, but then they sent me a lot of promotional content, from eBooks to videos. To clean up after I opted out of the service, I searched for all their emails and deleted them about a hundred at a time. Even by doing that, it took me a lot of time before I could clear out my inbox.

Turn Off Notifications

Some apps and services will send you notifications and reminders. Do you really need any of that? Turn off all notifications and then delete all email reminders of this type.

Set Up a Priority Inbox

If you're using Gmail, then you're missing out if you haven't used a priority inbox. No, you're not going to lose emails when you set it up. In fact, you will increase your productivity when you use it.

The priority inbox separates all the emails that you receive into separate categories. You have the important emails, starred, unread, and then finally everything else. I used to receive like 90 emails at the start of my day in the office.

That is like a ton of emails to sort through. After I turned the priority inbox on, I was able to spot the ten most important emails that needed my direct attention. I got more done for the day when I did that. When you turn this feature on, Gmail will sort your emails according to the sender and subject line.

To turn on your priority inbox, open your Gmail. And then, go to Menu (the hamburger icon), then Settings, your Account, Inbox Type, and then select Priority Inbox.

Allot Specific Times for Reading Emails

Treat your emails as part of your to-do list. Never prioritize going over your emails. In order for you to do that, you can set specific times when you should check your emails. As a rule of thumb, you don't want to check your inbox every hour.

You should limit the number of times you check it either once or twice a day. Some have experienced significant improvements in their productivity by simply checking their inbox at the start of the day and before leaving for home.

In the morning, they would choose one to five emails that they should respond to. The response should be quick. If an inter-office email was sent and it will take you five to ten minutes to write your response, then it would be better to walk over to your coworker's desk and talk about it.

I only view my inbox at 10 am. It isn't the first thing I do when I walk into my office. I usually have a to-do list prepared before the day ends, and that will be the first thing I would review as soon as I get to work.

I will then choose two to three tasks that would be my priority. And then I schedule them for that day. After I have allotted my time for each task, then I check my emails.

I only spend five to ten minutes and only read the most important ones. That's usually just one or two emails. If the tasks and topics under discussion in those emails can be squeezed in my schedule for that day, then I put it on my to-do list (i.e., I take a minute to compose a brief and concise response to those emails).

If there is something important, but it can't fit into my schedule for that day, then I put it on my to-do list for tomorrow. After that, I don't touch my inbox again for that day. I end up getting more things done for each day doing it that way.

Tip: Boomerang

If you're using Firefox or Google Chrome, then you might want to try the free plugin for these browsers called Boomerang. It's a useful tool that I found that helped me a lot when it comes to managing my emails.

Boomerang allows you to schedule an email that you can send a few days later, return an email into your inbox in case the person you emailed didn't reply after a few days, and set up other reminders to help you manage your email activities a lot better.

Another Tip: Use a Pomodoro Timer

We'll talk about the benefits of using a Pomodoro Timer later on. For now, just remember that you can use this timer (i.e., the tomato timer) to set a time limit for your email tasks.

This timer usually gives you 25 minutes to get everything done. After one Pomodoro is completed, you should be done with all your emails. If you're not done with one, or you still haven't gone over the rest of your emails, you should put them off for later in the afternoon.

Unsubscribe from the Majority of Email Lists

The emails from lists that you subscribed to are going to clog your inbox. You don't want to just delete them when you see them in your inbox because they will just keep coming every week.

What you should do is open one of them, scroll down, and check out the links. Find the one that unsubscribes you from that mailing list, and then follow the prompts to finally get you unsubscribed.

Do this for every email that you don't want to receive. Your mom's email doesn't count—okay? The more mailing lists that you signed up for, the longer it will take to get unlisted, but it will be worth the effort.

If you're not into the long and fun road of deleting and unsubscribing from email lists, there are apps that you can use to unsubscribe automatically. You just have to toggle the preferences and identify which emails you want to remove and retain.

Examples of these apps and tools are the following:

- Swizzle app for iOS
- Unroll.me
- Unlistr
- Unsubscriber

Remember to KISS

This is a fairly common acronym: KISS, and it stands for *keep it short and simple*. This also applies to emails that you send out. Remember to succinct when you write replies to emails.

What this means is that if you can say it in one or two sentences, then there is no point in trying to convey the same message in ten sentences. Keep your responses short. If they're asking about what time the meeting should be, you should state exactly what time. There is no need to beat around the bush.

Another thing to remember is that there is no need to ask questions of your own. If you do, you may end up replying back and forth in an email exchange, which basically wastes time. If you need to exchange emails, then call the other party instead. It makes the discussion faster and more efficient.

Don't Use Your Email as a Reminder

Some people use their emails as some sort of reminder—they send emails to themselves or ask their coworkers to send them emails to remind them of scheduled meetings and other events.

If you need reminders, then use your calendar. Use Google Calendar or other calendar software to set up reminders and other important items on your daily agenda.

If you're tired of sacrificing your productivity, wasting your time, or putting up with outrageous subject lines, the tips and tools mentioned here will be a big help. Your inbox should be treated as something sacred. It should only contain messages that are important and valuable to you.

Remember that you need to declutter your digital life from time to time. But if you follow the best practices mentioned here, everything will be made a lot easier.

Key Takeaways

- You will be doing a lot of digital inventories and decluttering
- Digital clutter tends to come up from time to time

- You need to declutter various aspects of your digital life and monitor your progress

Chapter 4: The Why and How of a Digital Detox

Detoxification is the process of removing toxic substances from the body. In cases of substance abuse, a person will have to go on a period of not taking the said substance (like alcohol, drugs, cigarettes, etc.). This period of abstention will allow the body to process the substances and clear the toxic influence.

That's basically the medical idea behind a detox. But what about a digital detox? It follows the same fundamental idea. When you do a digital detox, you will abstain from using any form of digital technology.

Does it sound scary? You're not going to use or even touch your phone for prolonged periods of time? Yes, it will be your phone, tablet, computer, TV, social media, the internet, and other forms of digital technology.

When you go through a detox of your digital life, you move your focus away from digital technology temporarily. You can then focus on real-world life from day to day. You will go

97

through face-to-face and in-person social interactions, and you can do it without any distractions. Think of it as a kind of sabbatical but shorter—like a digital timeout from all the tech-heavy things that you do.

It can be scary for some, yes. Now, before you decide whether it is something that you can do or not, please consider the benefits that you might gain from it. But before that, you should first ask what telltale signs indicate that you need a digital detox.

Signs That You Need a Digital Detox

Here is a summary of the different signs that you need to do a digital detox. We have mentioned some of them earlier in this book.

- You can't concentrate on one task for a long time. You feel the need to check your phone even for just a minute or two.
- You have this habit of staying up late just so you can play a game on your phone. Sometimes, you wake up early just to play.
- You can't go to sleep without playing on your phone before bedtime.

- You feel like you will be missing out on something if you don't check social media.

- You always check how many likes, shares, comments, and reactions there are on your posts.

- Sometimes after checking out your social media posts, you tend to feel angry, frustrated, depressed, or have some other negative effect on your feelings.

- The reverse may also be true—after you check your social media posts, you feel like you're complete and that you're ready to take on whatever task you have in line for that day.

- Not having your phone with you for a few minutes or hours makes you feel stressed or anxious. It feels like your phone (or some other device) is an important part of your person.

The FOMO Effect

FOMO is short for *fear of missing out*. It is a fear that people feel as if they are missing out on the best part or events of the day. They feel like they're not part of the collective whole of their friends, family, and colleagues if they don't take part in the latest trend, post, or share on social media.

It is as if they need to be part of the next big trending topic, or else they don't belong to the "in-crowd." What actually happens is that they are compelled to get constant connectivity.

If they are not connected, then they experience this fear. In fact, this fear is fed by that habit of being always connected to others through digital media. Without this constant connectivity (e.g., chat, posts, voice/video calls, etc.), they feel like their lives are less exciting.

There are times when you might feel overcommitting to social events, whether they are face-to-face meet-ups or digital meet-ups via Zoom, group chat, or whatnot. The overarching fear behind it all is that feeling of being left out.

No one wants to get left out, right? And that is why some people are compelled to stay connected online through digital media.

FOMO makes people check their phones, computers, or other digital devices constantly.

They don't want to miss out, and so they keep texting, direct messaging, and posting online.

A digital detox empowers you to set limits on the effects of FOMO. It doesn't mean that you are cutting yourself off completely from your digital world. What you're actually doing is giving yourself the reins as it were. You regain control over the choice when you check social media, and it's not your fear that will compel how often you need to do so.

Social Comparison in the Digital Age

Peer pressure is real in the digital age. Do you think peer pressure is only a high school thing? As it turns out, it has moved on to a wider plane of existence—the digital world. Sounds like *Dungeons and Dragons,* right? Think of it as a kind of metaphor.

Anyway, going back to the issue at hand—anyone who has spent time on social media has at least dwelled on comparing oneself to the quality of life your friends and family are showing on social media. You even compare yourself and how your life has been to strangers such as celebrities, some famous YouTuber, or some guy who is a friend of your friend whom you don't really know that is your age and maybe in the same line of work as you are.

Have you ever felt that these other guys are leading better and much more fulfilling lives than the one that you have right now? Just look at their latest picture carousel on Instagram. Look at the great vacations they have had—look at the places they've been. Look at their house, their pets, their car. They're doing better than you.

Now, before you follow that train of thought, remember this saying:

> *"Comparison is the biggest thief of your innermost joy in life."*

Doing a digital detox is a great way to take your mind off the comparison game, and focus on the life that you are currently blessed with and fortunate to have. It allows you to focus on what is important in your life without the need to compare yourself to others. In short, it allows you to be content about what you have right now and aspire for something better.

Impact on Work/Life Balance

Constant connectivity can have a strong impact on an individual's work-life balance. The level and amount of technology use play an important role in achieving that balance. Spending too much time with technology can make you feel overworked, feel job stress, and lose overall job satisfaction. This is according to a study published in the *Applied Research in Quality of Life Journal* [21].

Constant connectivity blurs out the boundaries between home life and work. You see, digital technology has made it very easy to check your emails, work files, text messages, and social media. A digital detox will allow you to create the necessary boundaries between work and your personal life. It can help reduce stress and allow you to focus on your family and personal life.

Mental Health Concerns

The daily heavy use of technology has been found to put people (especially young kids and adolescents) at risk for mental health issues, according to a study [22] that was published in *Child Development Journal.*

The study suggests that the more time you spend on digital technologies, the greater is your risk for conduct disorder and ADHD symptoms. In another study [23], it is suggested that too much social media increases symptoms of loneliness and depression.

The same study also suggests that by reducing social media use, people can reduce these symptoms. Doing a digital detox is a great way to reduce these symptoms.

Sleep Disruption

Do you often sleep with your phone right next to you or in bed? According to one study [24], using your phone prior to bedtime interferes with the quantity and quality of sleep. The same study suggests that it has a significant effect on children. It is further suggested that the heavy use of technology before sleeping is, in some way, connected to a higher body mass index.

Another study [25] says that using phones and other digital technology in bed greatly affects a person's mood. It also increases the likelihood of insomnia, anxiety, and shorter sleeping times.

Digital Technology Use and Stress

In the studies that we have cited so far, we can already see a pattern—the use of technology before bedtime and the overuse of the said technology can increase our stress levels. According to a survey published by the American Psychological Association, 18% of adults in the US indicated that one of the sources of significant stress in their lives is technology use. This includes constantly checking emails, text messaging, and social media use. The same findings were reaffirmed by a study [26] conducted by researchers from Sweden involving young adults.

The iPhone Effect

The overuse of smartphones reduces your ability to empathize with others. Experts dub this as the "iPhone Effect." According to one study [27], the mere presence of an iPhone or a smartphone can reduce the quality of your conversation with other people.

This happens even if you're not even using your phone while having a conversation with another person. The mere fact of holding the phone in your hand can induce such a response.

The solution is rather simple: leave your phone behind. Leave it in your bag and go to the water cooler and talk to a coworker. It will improve the quality of your interactions and help to return your ability to show empathy to other people.

Digital Detox: How to Do It

When it comes to how to do a digital detox, you will get a lot of different opinions and suggestions. Some will tell you that you need to abstain totally from any and all forms of digital media.

That would mean no cellphones ever, no emails, no social media, no internet, no TV, etc. It would be like living as if you were stranded all alone on a deserted island with no electricity whatsoever.

Of course, living like that will be almost impossible these days. You can't always stay in touch by physically visiting loved ones. Don't get me wrong, digital technology is useful, and it helps us to keep in touch with the people we care about and work with.

That is why I propose that digital minimalism should be one that focuses on purposeful use of technology, but not total abstinence. It should be a conscious mindful and willful use of digital media. There should be self-control applied to how we use them.

By detaching from digital devices, it will benefit our mental and emotional well-being. However, that doesn't mean when you do a digital detox, you will completely separate yourself from technology.

Just think about it, what if something wrong happens and you need to call 911? How do you do that if you cut off your home phone and throw away your smartphone? I believe that a digital detox should be more about setting boundaries and making use of digital devices and media in a way that benefits us.

Step 1: Be Realistic About What You Want to Do

If you can totally abstain from digital media and technology, then that would be great. If you can do it for just one day, then you will already get some kind of benefit from such a detox.

However, if you can't do it that long, then it's fine. If you can only partially detach from digital technology, then that is great too. But for a lot of people, a total separation from digital technology is impossible. Some of us rely on it to communicate with others, thus making it a necessity.

But that doesn't mean you can't go on a digital detox. You can still do it even if you're just limiting your use of your phone and other devices. The key here is to disconnect and abstain at times when it works well for your schedule.

If you need to use digital technology in your day-to-day life—for instance, you need it in your day job—then it is okay to use technology during the day. But since you don't need it as much after office hours, you should start by limiting your tech use by not checking your emails, no more

Facebook and other social media, and just limit your phone use to texts and phone calls.

Step 2: Set Up Limits to Digital Tech Use

You can use Spotify to play music while working and it is okay, even when you're doing a digital detox. As it was mentioned earlier, the important thing is to set limits to your digital use. I would recommend that you should limit your tech use to a bare minimum—only as necessary and nothing more.

One way to set limits to your use of digital media is by putting your devices on airplane mode. That way, your devices are disconnected from the internet and other wireless connections. You won't get distracted by online messages, texts, phone calls, app notifications, social media notifications, game announcements, and others.

You should also time your disconnects. As it was explained earlier, you should set what times you allow yourself to use digital media. If you do that, then you allow yourself to focus on other important matters like your personal space, health and fitness, family, hobbies, and other personal relationships.

Here are a few suggestions that you might want to try. Set limits to your digital technology use at the following times:

- Before you go to bed at night
- When you wake up in the morning
- When you're in a meeting
- When you're spending time with loved ones
- When you're catching up with friends
- When you're working on a project
- When you're spending time on your hobby
- When you're eating meals
- When you're dining with loved ones or other important people in your life

Step 3: Start Slow

You don't have to do it all in one day. Some people will find that quite difficult. You can start by reducing your social media usage by 30 minutes each day for a week. Research suggests that doing this will improve your quality of life by reducing depression symptoms and loneliness.

So, where do you find that 30 minutes of no social media time? You can start by not using your phone in bed before going to sleep. If using your phone at bedtime is a habit, you need to replace it with another habit. Instead of using your phone, read a book before going to bed.

Do all of that for about a week and try to make a habit out of it. If there were nights when you failed, then that is okay. Forgive yourself and try again the following night. You can also reschedule your 30-minute cellphone abstinence. If you missed it before bedtime, then you can do it during your morning routine—no smartphone use for 30 minutes in the morning—particularly during breakfast.

Step 4: Get Rid of Distractions

Now that you have reduced your smartphone use, you can start reducing your digital technology use a little bit more. You can continue by imposing no smartphone use during breakfast, lunch, and dinner.

You can take it up a notch by getting rid of distractions like push notifications, unnecessary alarms, and social media alerts. Turn them all off and keep only the really important ones.

Step 5: Set a Time for Social Media Use

Like I said earlier, digital technology has its uses—even social media. Social media is one way to connect and/or reconnect with friends and family—especially long lost ones. What you're trying to avoid when doing a digital detox is the overuse of social media.

Set certain times during the day when you can allow yourself to use social media. Let's say 30 minutes late in the morning and maybe 30 minutes at the end of the day when you get home. Think of it as your catch-up time with friends and family.

Step 6: Take It Up a Notch—Do a Digital Fast

Do steps 1 to 5 for several weeks. After you have gotten used to these new restrictions, you can step things up a notch by doing a complete digital fast for one whole day. You don't have to do it every day or every week. You can start by picking one day each month when you will do a digital fast—say the first day of each month—or maybe the first Sunday of each month—that way, you're not expecting any communication from work.

During your digital fast day, you're not going to touch or use any kind of digital technology. Think of it as your offline or unhooked day. It's just one day when you're totally disconnected from the internet and all kinds of digital media.

Step 7: Taking It Two Notches Up—Do a Digital Fast One Day Every Other Week

Now that you have tried to do a digital fast the previous month, it's time to move things up a little bit. This time, you're going to repeat step 6, but you're going to do it on the first and third Sunday of each month.

Step 8: Three Notches Up—Weekly Digital Fasts

This time you're going to do a digital fast one day each week. But there will be a little twist—you get to choose which day of each week you're going to do it. This will require a little more commitment.

Step 9: Fine-Tuning Things

By now, you have been doing a digital detox for quite a bit. You already know what it's like to disconnect and get more time for yourself. Now, it's time to fine-tune your efforts.

Notice that there are certain things that you do in your digital life that uses up a lot of time. Some people spend 11 hours each week on social media, which makes it a problematic habit.

It can be social media for some, but it may be *Fortnite* for others, and for others, it might be binge-watching TV shows on Netflix. It's different for everyone. To fine-tune your digital detox, determine how much time you spend on each of the digital media and technology.

Pick the one that you spend the most time on. Let's say it is *Fortnite*, and you spend four hours each night from 11 pm to 3 am playing it. Sometimes you do it on weekdays, but sometimes you do it on weekends.

What you can do is to reduce your *Fortnite* time. Let's say you make it a rule to stop playing *Fortnite* during business days (Monday to Friday). You will then restrict your use to the weekends since you don't need to report to work anyway.

Pick the app or device that you spend too much time on and reduce your usage.

Step 10: Reduce Social Media Time

People use social media all the time, even though we may be a bit shy to admit it. I'm not saying that you completely stop all forms of social media use. What I'm saying is that you should restrict your use of social media by reducing the number of social media platforms that you use to just one or two (Facebook and Twitter maybe). You can also reduce the amount of time you spend on social media using the strategies that we have discussed here.

More Digital Detox Tips

Here are some more that might be very helpful to you when you do a digital detox. Note that some people will find it easy to give up using their digital devices and tools, while others will find it a bit difficult. Sometimes, not using a smartphone even for just 24 hours can trigger anxiety in some people.

Each person is different, and sometimes people will need help and support to get it done. Try any of the following tips as you practice digital detoxes from time to time:

- Let your best friend, your spouse, other friends, and other family members know that you are doing a digital detox. This will remind them to not call, text, email, or send you online messages during your digital detox hours or days.

- Write down your progress in a journal. Someone once said that when effort is recorded, performance is increased. When your efforts are recorded and reported back to you, your success multiplies. One way to do just that is by recording your digital detox experiences in your journal and reading your journal at least once a week.

- Get out of the house—don't get stuck inside doing nothing. The idle mind is the devil's playground, as the adage goes. You will increase the level of temptation to use digital media when you're idle doing nothing, and you're all alone. Go out for a walk in the park, meet friends, have dinner with your special someone, go to the gym, take your dog out for a walk, go jogging, etc.

- Once you have opted to reduce the number of social media channels that you use, then you should make the ultimate step of deleting the apps you no longer use from your phone. For instance, you decided that you won't use Facebook anymore, then go ahead and delete the app from your phone. By doing that, you reduce the chances of getting tempted to sign in to your account.

- Try a new thing. For you to completely quit an old habit, you must replace it with a new one. For instance, you created a rule of not using your phone after 6 pm. That means your face shouldn't be buried in front of your computer screen after that time. You should find something else to do. Let's say you heard about a new sport like Brazilian Jiu-Jitsu, and it sounded interesting. What you should do is ***find a friend who will try BJJ with you*** and show up for class at 6 pm. <u>Doing it with another person and setting a time will help you form a new replacement habit a lot faster.</u>

Remember that you shouldn't rush your digital detox. Follow the tips mentioned here and take things slowly. If ever you find yourself succumbing to the temptation of using digital media for hours on end, then forgive yourself. After that, try again. Don't worry—it takes time for new habits to grow on you. The important thing is that you never give up.

Effects of Digital Detox on Your Brain

There was an experiment where entrepreneurs and neuroscientists were left in the Moroccan desert without any access to the internet. They underwent a short term digital detox, and the results were quite fascinating [27a].

Researchers reported that study participants were better able to create deeper and more meaningful personal connections. There is also a physiological benefit when the brain is no longer too focused on a small screen in your hand.

Participants reported reduced back and body pain. Their digestion also improved. Researchers attributed this to the fact that you no longer slouch and look down and thus improve your posture.

People were able to remember things a lot better simply because they were more present when interacting with others. Study participants were also sleeping better. This can be attributed to the fact that blue light from smartphones disrupts your circadian rhythm [27b]. By just doing a 24-hour digital detox, you greatly improve your sleep pattern. With the reduced blue light emissions, the brain is better able to signal the release of melatonin, which triggers sleep.

The benefits of digital detox were also reported in a study by the World Conference on

Technology, Innovation, and Entrepreneurship. In this study, students went through a short period of digital detox [27c].

The male students reported that they felt calmer and less stressed after a short-term digital detox. This meant a reduced production of cortisol in the brain and other parts of the body. The female students reported that they were better able to empathize with other students after participating in the experiment.

Another study [27d] suggests that a digital detox may help improve one's mood. Improving one's mood is only one of the benefits of short-term abstinence from digital technology. Studies suggest that it may help reduce anxiety [27e], better manage depression symptoms, and may help relieve eating disorders [27f].

Ways Your Life Can Improve After Digital Minimalism

Here are some of the immediate benefits of undergoing a digital detox. Consider it as your first brush with digital minimalism.

Allow me to list some of the benefits that you can get out of such an experience.

1. *You Identify Which Technology is Essential and Which Ones are Just Fluff*

The very first benefit that you will get out of digital minimalism is that you will know which digital media and technology are essential. You will learn to clean up your computer and your phone, and your devices will run more efficiently. Apart from that, you will also work more effectively and get your life straightened out.

2. *You Learn to Control Your Use of Digital Technology*

When you have identified what pieces of technology are essential to you and your work, you will be able to focus on those tools. You choose how and when to use digital resources; you will use them to their utmost potential.

You don't need to run one hundred apps on your computer and your phone. You only need a handful or less, and you maximize the usefulness of each one. You also save money on the side because you reduce the monthly subscriptions that you have to pay.

3. You Become More Productive

This is related to the previous two points mentioned here. You become more productive because you are no longer distracted by hundreds of notifications. You don't need to pay attention to a dozen different work tools.

For example, if you're a graphic designer, you don't need to jump from GIMP to Photoshop, to Canva, to Pixlr X, and other tools. You just pick one or two, and that's it. You increase your productivity and spend less time at work and get more time for yourself.

4. You Don't Feel Overwhelmed

Do you remember the last time you cleaned up your room and organized your mess? Everything was so tranquil, peaceful, and you felt calmer, right? That's about the same thing you will get after doing a digital detox and practicing digital minimalism.

You no longer have any work backlogs, you don't have a ton of emails to respond to, you don't have a pile of reports you need to review. Everything runs smoothly, and there's no need to rush.

5. You're No Longer Distracted

One expert was on the button when he said that scrolling through endless posts, videos, pictures, and shopping items on your phone's screen is the new way we smoke cigarettes.

We have all mindlessly scrolled through our feeds. Don't worry; even I am guilty of doing that as well. You get distracted by the many notifications, and before you know it, you're halfway through your day, and you have accomplished very little.

The good news is that after doing a digital detox and practicing digital minimalism for at least a couple of weeks, you will feel less distracted, and you will have a renewed sense of purpose. You will know exactly what it is you want to do and when you need to get it all done.

Key Takeaways

- There are signs that you can use to determine whether you need a digital detox
- Digital addiction has many negative impacts, including those on our mental health

- You can reduce your stress levels, get better sleep, and get better focus when you do a digital detox
- Digital minimalism brings a lot of benefits such as better mental clarity, being less distracted, and you regain control over the technology you want to use

Chapter 5: Digital Mindfulness

Digital mindfulness is the application of mindfulness practices in your digital life. It involves the creation of structure and routines when it comes to your use of digital technology. Mindfulness is one of the tools that you can use to eliminate interruptions and distractions.

What Is Mindfulness?

Mindfulness is both a psychological process and also a state of mind when you are conscious of the present moment. You achieve it by focusing on the things that are currently happening around you. At the same time, you are also calmly and consciously accepting your thoughts, sensations, and feelings as you become aware of them.

It is something that you have done from time to time, whether you were aware of it or not. Mindfulness is also used as a therapeutic practice that allows people to relax.

At its core, mindfulness involves the acceptance of your memories, feelings, and thoughts minus any judgment on yourself or others because of those things. You will allow these experiences to come along and then just observe them. There will be no judgment whether they are good or bad thoughts, memories, and feelings.

You also do not rehearse the past as you live in the moment. In a mindful state, you also do not focus or imagine the future or its possibilities.

Origins of Mindfulness Practice

Mindfulness has deep roots in Buddhism. Buddhists have practiced it for hundreds of years. However, you don't have to believe in Buddhist teachings to enable you to practice mindfulness and mindfulness meditation.

Mindfulness as a practice (and not just the meditation part) reached the Western world through the efforts of Jon Kabat-Zinn. He was a Professor of Medicine Emeritus at the University of Massachusetts Medical School. He later founded the Mindfulness in Medicine, Health Care, and Society.

He also founded the Stress Reduction Clinic, where he introduced the Stress Reduction and Relaxation Program. In his work, he removed the Buddhist framework in his practice, taking away any religious aspects of his clinical practice. He then reformulated and renamed his stress reduction program as Mindfulness-Based Stress Reduction, or MBSR.

By distancing his practice from traditional Buddhist teachings, Kabat-Zinn was able to put mindfulness practice into mainstream clinical practice. Today, mindfulness is recognized as an effective therapeutic tool.

Studies [28] show that meditation, specifically mindfulness meditation, induces the brain to create new gray matter and improves its plasticity. This is one of many studies that have shown how useful mindfulness meditation is.

How Mindfulness Can Help You: Two Key Points

According to Kabat-Zinn himself, mindfulness is:

"...a means of paying attention in a particular way; on purpose, in the present moment, and nonjudgmentally."

Two main key points should be emphasized here when it comes to mindfulness as a practice before you can use it in digital minimalism. The first point is that you must learn to do things on purpose.

The opposite of mindfulness is mindlessness, which means you do things automatically or reactively. When something happens, you automatically follow or use a pre-programmed response.

For instance, if you have used your phone as a habitual escape from boredom and sadness, then whenever you feel bored or sad, the first thing that you will do, without thinking about it, is reach for your phone.

Some might think that this is a rather quick solution to boredom, loneliness, and all those negative feelings. But there is a problem with this automatic and technology-dependent response— what if the next time you grab your phone to check your email, social media, etc., you get a negative response—the news or posts are negative?

People don't like your posts. Someone even disliked the video or picture you posted. Someone even made a critical comment about it—and mentioned you as well. Instead of solving your problems, it caused more problems in return.

You find nothing interesting to watch on YouTube or Netflix. There is nothing to catch up on. There are no trends to follow. Instead of helping you find peace, you find more boredom and more stress.

The solution that mindfulness provides is purposeful and intentional choice. By doing things on purpose, you regain the power to choose and human agency. You do not only regain the power to choose how to get rid of boredom, loneliness, and stress, but you also are empowered to choose how to respond to the stimuli behind such feelings. You tackle the root cause of the problem and not just treat the symptoms.

The other key, according to Kabat-Zinn, is going through the experience non-judgmentally. When you feel bored, you will learn to acknowledge the experience. But you won't judge whether that experience is a bad one or a good one.

When you are mindful, you are in the zone. You are in control. You feel sadness because of a memory that came to you because of a post on social media. You feel it, and you do feel sad, but you choose not to be affected by it because you did not judge it as a negative or positive influence for you at that moment.

All you ever do in a state of mindfulness is to go through the experience and let it flow. These feelings, memories, and experiences come and go. And when, after they have passed, then you are still you. You are in control, and you no longer need to be depressed because you choose not to.

As you learn more about mindfulness and practice it in your daily life, you will become more aware of what's going on in your inner world—your inner dialogue. It's this internal monologue that pushes you to grab your digital technology (phone, Alexa speaker, TV, etc.).

According to best-selling author Stephen Covey, there is a brief time and space between stimulus and response. When something triggers a reaction from you, for a brief moment, you have a choice about what to do.

Reactive people tend to use a habitual response (e.g., use their phone, check social media, listen to sad music, etc.). But a non-reactive person (aka one who is proactive) will recognize that brief moment between stimulus and response. They will use that short moment to choose how they will respond.

Practicing mindfulness allows you not only to recognize that brief moment between stimulus and response, but you also get to expand it. By practicing mindfulness, you regain that inner strength and empowerment. You no longer have that need to check your emails every hour, hoping that you will find something interesting.

You will no longer be affected by what people post on social media. Even if people don't react to your posts and even dislike them, you do not feel sad, angry, or resentful. You choose how to respond to such things. They don't like your photo? It's okay. You move on. What's important is that you did something that you felt was important to you regardless of how people reacted to it.

You never get robbed of your satisfaction, contentment, or even your sense of hope. Remember that the ultimate goal in mindfulness practice in the digital world is to allow you to slow down and fully experience life as it happens.

We have become so acclimated to a fast-paced environment that we have failed to fully live. Digital mindfulness is not about avoiding the negative things in life. That is utterly impossible. Bad things happen all the time, and good things happen all the time too.

What you will learn through mindfulness practice is that you can live in those situations and still be okay—still in control. You regain the power to learn from these experiences and healthily cope with the negative.

Mindfulness will teach you to be aware of all your emotions. By being aware of them and understanding them, you learn to cope with the things that you used to avoid. Eventually, it teaches you how to specifically deal with the future negativity that may come into your life.

Finally, digital mindfulness brings you peace of mind in an ever-changing and increasingly connected world.

Practicing Mindfulness in the Digital Age

Some people see digital mindfulness as the antidote to digital distraction. I would rather prefer to think of it as one of many tools that you can use. It's not the secret formula or secret sauce to overcoming digital technology addiction. It's not the only thing that you need to do for digital minimalism.

Now, without diving directly into the practice of mindfulness and mindfulness meditation, here are a few things that you can do right now that will set you up for digital mindfulness.

We'll start with some tips and then cover several mindfulness meditation and practices that you can do.

Track Your Screen Time

Tech companies today like Google and Apple have acknowledged that smartphone addiction is a real thing. That is why they have introduced tools that users and subscribers can take advantage of in order to manage their screen time.

Apple has included the Screen Time app to its iOS suite, and for its part, Google has created Digital Well-Being Tools. These tools can help you monitor how much time you have spent looking at your phone's screen. They can also show you how many times you have unlocked your phone, how many notifications you have seen, what tools and pages you have viewed like Chrome, Facebook, messaging, Instagram, games, etc.

What you can do is to install these screen time apps on your phone and monitor how much time you have spent on your device. Set a limit for yourself for each day. How many times do you want to unlock your phone, how many notifications are your maximum each day, and how many hours of screen time is your limit?

Once you have reached any of these limits, then you must resolve not to touch or use your phone again until the following day.

Stop All Non-Human Notifications

Notice that a lot of the notifications that you get in your computer, phone, or other devices are automatic. That means they are pre-programmed. There is no human being that sent it to you on purpose. The AI behind these programs or apps sent them because certain conditions have been met in their programming, and thus they sent these notifications to you.

For instance, YouTubers usually tell you to like and subscribe to their channels, right? They also tell you to click the bell button. By clicking that, you get automatic notifications. It's not like the person who owned that channel intentionally sent you a notification that they have a new video uploaded.

The notification was sent to your device because the owner of that channel uploaded something new. Do you really need to view the said video right away? The answer is no, you don't need to see it right away. But you were notified, and eventually, you got distracted.

The same is true for other apps. Allowing automatic notifications by different apps will prompt you now and then. Sometimes, when a timed event in a game has started, then you will get notified.

Here's what you should do: turn off all notifications. You can keep notifications sent by actual human beings like emails from your coworkers. But turn off all the notifications from installed apps. Of course, you can keep the ones that you need, such as notifications from your calendar and the ones from your alarm clock.

Switch to Do Not Disturb Mode

Check if your phone has a do not disturb mode or quiet mode. It most likely will have that setting. When you're in work mode, when you're teaching a class, when you're talking to your spouse, having a meal with your family, playing music, having a one-on-one talk with someone, when you're sleeping, when you're doing anything important, keep your phone in another room.

That way, you can concentrate on the thing that you were doing. If that is not possible, then switch on the do not disturb mode and keep your phone in your bag—not in your pocket, not on your person. Put it in your bag and close your bag so you forget that you had your phone in there.

Charge Your Phone Outside of the Bedroom

We all put our phones on a table nightstand when we go to sleep so it will be within easy reach. Chances are your phone will need charging before you go to bed at night. So you keep on the nightstand or bedside table while it's charging.

Here's a quick tip—charge your phone outside the bedroom. That way, you won't be tempted to grab it while you're lying in bed.

But you need your phone since you use it as your alarm, right? Switch to a regular alarm clock. It performs the same task—it wakes you up with that annoying racket first thing in the morning. It even has one advantage when it comes to digital minimalism—it doesn't have internet.

The same rule applies to your smart speakers, smart assistants, and other digital tools. Alexa can still hear you even if your Echo Dot 3rd Gen is outside your door—yes, that's how powerful those new microphones are.

Do a Digital Detox Once a Week

In the previous chapter, we talked about doing a digital detox. To help you practice digital mindfulness, you should do at least one day of complete digital detox each week. Pick a day when you can and want to disconnect and live 24 hours completely off the grid. You don't need to leave your home, just disconnect everything and turn the WiFi off. If you need to review the information on how to do a digital detox, then please review the discussion in chapter 6.

Go On an Off-Grid Vacation

Plan to go on an off-grid vacation with your entire family. You can also use it to spend time with your closest friends. It can be for a week or two. If you have enough leave credits (or if your boss grants you a month-long vacation or more), then you should plan on going off-grid for a month.

You don't need to leave the country. You can even vacation somewhere else in the next town if there's a nature park or some other place where you can stay. Enjoy the outdoors and learn to do things without digital technology. If you need to make a call, use the regular landline phone or a payphone.

Use this moment to spend some quality time with the people who mean the most to you.

Take Mindful Moments before Jumping Into a Task

Before you start any task—taking calls, calling clients, sending emails, editing videos, starting a video meeting, writing a function in the program that you were writing, etc. You should take a moment to be mindful. Don't just jump into the task and hack into it like crazy.

Take a moment to remind yourself of what you're supposed to do. Take five slow deep breaths. And then go to work. Avoid the rush so that you prevent your mind from going into autopilot mode.

Mindful Waiting

In our fast-paced work environment, we tend to multitask when there is a bit of wait time in one part of our work. For instance, when a page we're trying to open starts to lag, we tend to open another tab on our browsers to check a different page for a different task.

Whenever this happens, we lose focus on the original task that we intended to do. We have our attention divided, and eventually, we get fewer things done. We think we are multitasking, but we're not.

Multitasking is a myth [29], and researchers and experts confirm this fact. What we human beings are actually doing is task-switching. We switch from one task to the other rather quickly. But that doesn't mean we can do both tasks efficiently.

We sort of trick our minds that we are multitasking. Research confirms that people can hardly concentrate on two tasks done at the same time. This means that if you want to get things done quickly and more efficiently, you should focus on only one task at a time.

The reason why people can't multitask is the interference between two or more tasks. The brain starts to struggle when you pay attention to two or more things at the same time.

That is why instead of going into multitasking mode when you are made to wait, take the time to do a short mindfulness exercise. We will go over several mindfulness exercises in the next section of this chapter. Just remember that whenever you hear the queue music, don't grab your phone. Use that time to meditate and practice mindfulness.

Focus on One Task at a Time

As was explained earlier, trying to focus on a task is an inefficient way to get things done. Whenever you are tempted to multitask, take a moment to decide whether you can finish one task more efficiently and then moving on to the next. This will allow your mind to remain calm and clear instead of being stressed out while trying to do a balancing act moving from one task to the next. Unit tasking is usually the better option, all things considered.

Do Mindful Moments in Transition

We usually jump from one task to the next as if we are in a hurried flight to get everything done. In the frenzy, we sometimes fail to notice the increasing amount of tension and stress because of the workload that is given to us.

To prevent this from happening, you should do mindful transitions every time you complete a task. For instance, after completing one of the items on your to-do list, instead of just moving on to the next item on that list, you should pause and perform a short mindfulness exercise.

Note that this will be the first of the different exercises that we will go over in a little bit:

1. Be still.
2. Close your eyes.
3. Take three slow and deep breaths.
4. Pay attention to how your lungs feel as you take each deep breath.

5. As you exhale, try to recall where you are and what you have just finished.

6. Pay attention to how you feel right now— do you feel cold, relieved, still tense?

7. Let all of that feeling wash away as you release each deep breath.

8. Open your eyes and move on to the next task.

Note that it only takes a few seconds to do the exercise described above. You can do this exercise quickly before you answer a client call, walk into your office, get out of the car after arriving at an appointment, and any other time when you need a few seconds of mental clarity.

Must-Know Mindfulness Exercises

The following are mindfulness exercises that everyone must know, especially if you're trying to learn how to practice digital minimalism. These exercises will teach your mind how to be in the present moment. They will help you enter into a state of calm, something that you will need to sort through any kind of chaos that might be happening in your life right now.

Body Scan Exercise

The body scan method is one of the first mindfulness exercises that will be taught to people who want to learn mindfulness meditation. In this exercise, you will learn how to systematically focus your attention.

Don't worry—it is a very simple exercise. Doing a body scan gives you that rare opportunity to become aware of your body, and experience it as it is with no judgments. No judgment will be passed on the state of your body, and you won't even have to try and change anything.

It will also teach you to be aware of possible sources of bodily tension, discomfort, and pain. The body scan exercise is designed to counteract any resentments and negative feelings you may have towards your body.

In time, you will learn to be more aware of your body's needs. You will become more present with its needs and sensations. It will help you make healthier decisions about exercise, sleep, and eating habits.

According to one study [30], it is suggested that people who regularly perform body scans can reduce their stress levels and improve their psychological well-being.

How to do it:

A full body scan will require up to 20 to 45 minutes. However, you can do shorter sessions that range from one minute to 15 minutes. A body scan can be done lying down, sitting on a chair, standing up, or even while walking, albeit slowly at first.

Remember that if anything should distract you while doing a body scan, you should just observe the distraction, forgive yourself for getting distracted, and then return your focus to that part of your body that you were paying attention to.

No judgments—remember that distractions like feelings, memories, sounds, and others are just passing and fleeting experiences. They have no power over you. Observe and then let them pass. Go back to your body scan.

Here's how you get started:

1. Choose a position that is most comfortable for you (i.e., sitting down, lying in bed, or standing up).

2. Start the meditation by paying attention to your entire body.

3. Close your eyes if it helps you visualize the condition of your body.

4. If you are seated, pay attention to the feeling of your body's weight on the chair. If you're lying down, pay attention to your body's weight on the surface you're lying on. In case you're standing, pay attention to the feeling of the weight of your body on your feet.

5. Take a few slow deep breaths.

6. Notice how deep the air enters your body and the tension that comes with it that you feel in your lungs.

7. Notice the relaxed feeling you get as you exhale the air emptying your lungs.

8. Now, place your attention on your feet and legs.

9. Pay attention to the feelings in your feet— is there any tension? If there is, then try to relax your feet. Take a deep breath.

10. Focus your attention on your legs, knees, and thighs. Release any tension in these parts of your body and relax them. Take a deep breath.

11. Move your attention to your hips and buttocks. Are the muscles and tissues there tense? Relax and then take a deep breath.

12. Move your focus to your stomach area next. Relax any muscles that are too tense. And then take a deep breath.

13. Do the same for your chest and back. Pay attention to the feeling of your body pressed against any surfaces, if any. Relax your muscles in these parts. Take a slow, deep breath.

14. Focus your attention on your neck and throat. Allow them to relax.

15. Move up to your jaw and soften that part of your body. Pay attention to the sensations you have on your face. Relax any facial muscles that are currently tense. There is no need to smile, frown, or have any other facial expressions at this time. Take a slow, deep breath.

16. This time, allow yourself to focus on the sensations that are being experienced by your entire body. Allow your body to experience them and then let your body relax.

17. Take several deep breaths and when you're ready, open your eyes and get on with your day.

Note that a shorter body scan session will only give you enough time to focus your attention on one or two parts of your body. You get to choose which part you want to focus on.

Mindful Breathing Exercise

This is another basic mindfulness exercise, and it is also one of the first exercises to be taught to beginners. Mindful breathing is a great way to relieve yourself of anger, stress, and anxiety. After doing this exercise, you will feel that your powers of better judgment will return, your skills and capabilities will reset, and you will regain your ability to pay attention and focus on things.

You can say that mindful breathing is a foundational exercise that will be used in pretty much every kind of mindfulness exercise. If you noticed, you were already performing mindful breathing in the previous exercise (i.e., body scan).

Mindful breathing distances you from your feelings and your thoughts. You begin to realize that your feelings and experiences may be part of you, but they do not define who you are.

This distancing from your personal experiences empowers you to tolerate the negative things that happen to you. Mindful breathing allows your mind to anchor onto something (i.e., your breathing).

You have something to focus on and thus separate yourself from emotions and thoughts. You stay present and become aware of the present moment. You do not get distracted from drastic decisions and actions that you might regret later.

In one study [31], researchers suggest that people who perform mindful breathing or focused breathing become better at regulating their emotions.

How to Do It

Mindful breathing can be done in two to 15 minutes, depending on how much time you have. Experts suggest that you should perform this exercise at least once a day. The more frequently you do this exercise, the better you will be at focusing your mind and remain more mindful.

Here's how you can do it:

1. Find a nice, comfortable, quiet place where you can relax and sit down. You can sit on a chair or just sit on the floor—if you're sitting on the floor, please find some kind of cushion to sit on since you may end up sitting in that area for an extended period of time. Your tongue should be placed on the roof of your mouth. You can place your hands on your lap, on the chair, or anywhere you like.

2. Give yourself a few seconds to get comfy where you're sitting. Be mindful of the feelings that you experience. Allow these feelings to come and go.

3. Now, begin your mindful breathing. Breathe in and pay attention to the feeling of the air rushing into your lungs.

4. You don't need to breathe in any way. Just breathe as you usually do. It can be a short breath, a deep breath, or even a rapid shallow breath.

5. As you breathe, notice how it feels to have the air pass your nose, mouth, throat, neck, and finally into your lungs.

6. Try to notice how one breath ends and how the next one begins. Follow the rhythmic pattern of your breathing.

7. If anything like memories, feelings, sounds, or anything that you sense tries to take your focus away from your breathing, give it a moment and allow it to pass. Forgive yourself if you got distracted and go back to focusing on your breathing.

8. Repeat steps 1 to 7 as long as you like. It's all up to you. The important point is that you are able to maintain your focus on your breathing.

9. Keep breathing, and appreciate what you have accomplished at this time. Now you can get up and go back to life in general.

Walking Meditation Exercise

Walking meditation is one of the methods that you can practice mindfulness even when you're on the go. After practicing mindful breathing and body scans several times, you can now try doing walking meditations.

When you do walking meditations, your attention and focus will be on the actual physical experience. It is something that we have taken for granted. When you go on this meditative walking exercise, you will pay attention to every movement that you make when you take every step.

According to one study [32], incorporating mindful walking in your daily routine can help reduce stress, improve mental conditions, fight depression, and relieve physical symptoms due to medical conditions such as heart disease.

How to Do It

For you to enjoy the full benefits of meditative walking, you should do this exercise at least ten minutes each day for an entire week. The more times you do it, the easier it will be for you to enter into a mindful state in your everyday life.

1. The first step is to find a nice quiet place where you can walk back and forth without any distractions. This is important if you haven't done mindful walking or meditative walking before.

   You don't need a very long lane to walk on, and you don't even need a specific place to go to. A quiet lane on your block that is usually free of traffic will be great. You can even do it indoors if you like to avoid a lot of distractions too. If you do it outdoors, just make sure that there won't be anyone there to stop you or grab your attention. Now, move on to the next step.

2. Take 10 to 15 steps forward on the pathway that you have chosen. After completing the required number of steps, pause for a bit, and then take a deep breath.

3. Now, turn back and then walk the other way. When you reach the other end, pause and then take a deep breath.

4. Now that you have walked back and forth at least once in both directions, the next time you walk back, pay attention to each step that you take.

5. Focus on how you lift your foot, take a step, how well your foot lands on the ground, how you move your weight forward, how your body swings as you take each step, and how your arms move while walking.

6. When you take each step, it doesn't have to be done in a very fast manner. In fact, you should take a slow walk so that you can easily observe how you take each step.

7. Don't take large steps, take small shorter steps. Make it a relaxed stroll, one that is unhurried.

8. If you want, you can clasp your hands in front of you or behind you so that you can concentrate only on the movement of your feet—which makes observing your body's motions a lot easier.

9. Notice that your mind will eventually wander as you walk back and forth. It's okay; it's very natural for all of us to do that. When your mind gets distracted, forgive yourself, and then go back to observing and focusing on the motions of your body as you take a relaxed stroll.

10. After you have felt that you have done enough walking and achieved a complete awareness of your body's movements, you can stop, take a deep breath, and then go back to whatever it was that you were doing.

Do walking meditations every day for a week. After that, you can try to do it every time you have a chance to walk.

Raisin Method

We sometimes do things automatically with no thought about what we are about to do. Many times during the day, we go into a mindless auto mode where we follow a habitual chain of reactions and do things using preconditioned responses.

For example, when you hear your phone ringing, you instinctively reach for it and answer it, giving no thought about the wonderful technology that you have in your hands. The cheeseburger you ordered has been served; you instinctively dig in, go on bite after bite, have a conversation about something with your friend, and before you know it, you are done with your meal.

Did you notice the power of your mobile device? Did you notice how well-made your sandwich was? This exercise will help you make mindfulness an automatic habit. You will learn to take notice of the little things and appreciate the little things in life.

This mindfulness exercise will require a prop—a box of raisins. What if you don't have raisins? Then you can use some other treat. Choose something small, not so filling, and healthy. This exercise also teaches you to engage your different bodily senses.

It is recommended that you take five minutes each day to do this meditative exercise. Here are the steps:

1. First step: Hold one raisin gently in the palm of your hand.
2. Look at the raisin in your hand. You can hold it in between two fingers if you want to just let you see its features.
3. Pay attention to how it feels in your hand. Is it rough, smooth, hard, or soft? Pay attention to how its folds and ridges look like. Hold it up against the light and see the kind of shadow it makes. If you look at it with the light shining behind it, can you see the silhouette of its internal parts?
4. How much do you think it weighs?
5. Turn the raisin over between your fingers and explore how it feels. How do you describe its texture? You might want to close your eyes so that you can visualize its surface texture.

6. Smell the raisin. How does it smell? Do you remember smelling that sort of scent when you eat foods that use raisins as an ingredient?

7. Close your eyes. Now place the raisin in between your lips, but don't put it in your mouth.

8. Did you notice that? Notice how your hand knows exactly where your mouth is. You don't think about it; you never estimated the exact distance your hand had to travel and the exact placement of your mouth in relation to your face. You were aware of exactly where to put that raisin so that it will reach your lips. On top of that, your lips also know exactly how much pressure should be applied to the raisin so that it won't fall to the floor. Your spatial awareness is something that you have taken for granted, and now you are re-experiencing it all over again.

9. Next, put the raisin in your mouth. But don't swallow it. Take your time and chew it slowly. Pay attention to the flavors that you taste in your mouth. If one raisin is not enough to allow you to taste the actual

flavor of a raisin, then eat another one (or two). Chew slowly and try to describe the taste in your mouth.

10. Finally, swallow the raisin. How does it feel as it slowly makes its way into your stomach?

This raisin method can actually be used as a mindful eating exercise. When you use this process to mindfully eat your meals, you should pay attention to the look of the food that was served on your plate, how it feels when you cut it into bite-size pieces, how it smells, and the effect of the flavors in your mouth.

Self-Compassion Method

Do you often relive past mistakes? Did you ever say things that you regret saying? We all have regrets—we regret wrong decisions, bad moves, wrong things we did to others, poor judgment, and a lot of other things that we may have directly or indirectly caused.

We rehash the past and fail to find joy in the present, and thus we think our futures are clouded. Yes, it sounds like something mystical or even Buddhist, but these observations have roots in our present experience even in our modern day.

This exercise will allow you to focus or center on a single tangible object. You will use it to channel your focus and come to a realization about your past experiences and your current state of awareness.

This mindfulness exercise will allow you to take a break when you tend to beat yourself up for past faults and mistakes. Instead of using harsh self-criticism, you will practice a healthier response—a compassionate response.

The following exercise will walk you through all the essential components of compassion towards self. You will learn how to be mindful, be kind to yourself, and have that feeling of common humanity (elements defined by Kristin Neff Ph.D., University of Texas).

Here's how you can do it:

This exercise requires only five minutes of your time. You can do this exercise every time you feel that stress is building up, and if your memories are starting to haunt you at any time of the day. But for starters, you can just do it once a week.

1. Find a quiet place where you can sit down and be alone with your thoughts. Get comfy, and start breathing slowly. Be mindful of each breath you take.

2. As you sit there paying attention to your breath, think of a situation that you are going through. Choose the toughest one that you are facing right now.

3. As you recall that problem or situation, try to notice if you feel any sense of emotional or actual physical discomfort. You will usually manifest a symptom like butterflies in your stomach, sweat, feeling cold, despair, or some other feeling.

4. Now, acknowledge that experience by saying, "I am suffering from this right now." There is no need to judge the situation as either good or bad for you. Tell yourself what you feel—"it hurts" or "I feel stressed," etc.

5. Next, point out to yourself that the experience of difficulty and pain is a common experience for all human beings. You can do that by saying to yourself, "This suffering is part of my human life." You can also say, "I am not alone; there are others who are also going through the same problems that I am going through." The important thing in this step is that you acknowledge that your suffering is not unique and that other people have or are currently going through the same level or amount of suffering.

6. Place your hands close to your heart, or you can even just give yourself a tight hug. Say to yourself, "May I offer kindness to myself" or some other similar phrase. Examples of similar phrases are "May I always be forgiving to myself," "May I always be patient with myself," "May I learn to accept me for who I truly am," "May I always be strong no matter what," and others. You get to choose the phrase

depending on the dilemma or situation that you are currently encountering.

You can perform this five-minute exercise of self-kindness at night before going to bed, when you wake up first thing in the morning, or any time when you find an extra five minutes during your day. The important thing is that you can find time to be compassionate to yourself.

Meditation for Extending Kindness

In the previous mindfulness exercise, you learned how to express self-compassion for five minutes. In this exercise, you will be doing it for 15 minutes. However, there is also an added twist: you will be extending kindness and compassion to others as well.

Experts say that people who are kind to others tend to be more satisfied with their lives. They also have better relationships with others. This type of mindfulness meditation is also called metta meditation, and it can increase your natural capability to be kind to other people despite the situation you find yourself in.

How you can do it:

This form of meditation will be similar to the previous mindfulness exercise. This exercise was developed originally by Stanford University's Science Director, Emma Seppala. You can learn more about its benefits and download guided meditation audio from Dr. Seppala's website [33].

There are two phases of this exercise. The first one is to receive kindness and compassion and be aware of all that you have received. The second one is to send it out to others so that you may bless others as well.

Receiving Loving Kindness

1. Find a nice comfortable place where you can sit down. Lean back on a chair's backrest and then close your eyes. Take several deep breaths until you are completely relaxed. You will go through several visualizations, so keep your eyes closed throughout this exercise.

2. Think of someone very close to you— someone you hold dear to your heart. It

should be someone you know who loves you very much. It can be a deceased parent, the person mentoring you right now, your best friend, your spouse, your children, your grandparents who died when you were a kid, etc.

3. Select one of those people who love you and imagine that person sitting right beside you right now. Imagine that person giving you a warm, reassuring hug, a pat on the back, or other means of expressing their love to you.

4. Take note of the warm, loving feeling that you are experiencing because of that love that is extended to you.

5. Think of another person, and have that person also sit beside you on the other side. Imagine that person also extending his or her love to you. Now you have three people in your huddle.

6. Pick another person who loves you and imagine that person also expressing his or her love to you.

7. Add another person in the loving circle that you are experiencing right now. And then add another, and another, until you

have several friends and loved ones who are showing you their compassion and love.

8. Focus on the loving feeling that you are experiencing at that moment.

Radiating Kindness

1. Now that you know what it feels like to receive compassion and kindness from those who truly loved you, it is time for you to return that kindness and compassion.

2. Go back to the first person you imagined or remembered. Imagine giving back that love and compassion to that person. You may say things like, "Thank you for your kindness. May you be happy and live with ease."

3. Repeat the same steps for every single person in your loving huddle.

4. After you're done reciprocating the love you have felt to everyone in your huddle, think of someone who you do not know well—maybe just an acquaintance—and then send that same love to that person.

Think two more acquaintances and try to imagine how it would feel like when you express your appreciation and love for them.

5. Now, it is time to extend the reach of your compassion. Imagine people around the world who may not be as fortunate as you. Imagine extending your love to them. Say words like, "I wish you live well, happy, and in good health." Imagine being able to help those people in your own little way.

6. Take three slow, deep breaths. And when you are ready, open your eyes.

Take note of how you feel after this exercise. Remember the state of your mind after feeling love and expressing it to others. You can always come back to this experience during the day, especially when times are rough.

How to Help Your Family Practice Digital Mindfulness

The next questions are, when will you use these mindfulness exercises, and how do you teach them to your family? If not your family, then maybe your coworkers or your team in the office; there will always be people to whom you can share the benefits of mindfulness applied in the digital age.

You can use these mindfulness exercises whenever you have idle time. Instead of grabbing your phone and playing a game or maybe scanning through social media, you can replace such activities with a mindfulness exercise.

Remember that the choice is always yours. Do you want some quick satisfaction that comes from your digital device, or do you prefer the lasting peace of mind that you can get from the practice of digital mindfulness? You can only say that practicing mindfulness is the better option after you have tried the exercises that have been described in detail above.

Here's a **big TIP**: Choose mindfulness every time you are presented with a choice between opening an email, watching a video on YouTube, checking social media, or using your phone. The long-term benefits of better focus, peace of mind, reduced stress, and mental clarity is so much better.

Tips on Practicing Digital Mindfulness in the Home

It is one thing to practice mindfulness yourself, but it is another to get your spouse and your kids to do it too. The first step to teaching mindfulness to your loved ones is to practice digital mindfulness first yourself. Once you have tried it, you can inform your family about what you're doing and ask for their support.

Talk to them about it and share your experiences. Tell them about the benefits that you have enjoyed from practicing digital mindfulness. The next person you want to get on board with the practice is your spouse.

Both of you should then set the example for your kids. You can then have a family meeting and get your kids to practice it also. Remember to relate to them the benefits, and reassure them that as parents, you are doing it for their welfare.

Now, here are a few ideas on how you can practice digital mindfulness at home and teach it to your children.

1. Set Up Family Mindfulness Challenges

Kids love challenges, and they love the rewards that come with their efforts. You may have been modeling how mindfulness is done. You may have even asked your kids to try one of the exercises described above. They may already have a bit of an idea about what mindful living is like.

You can have some family fun doing mindfulness challenges. For instance, you can teach a short mindful breathing exercise to your kids, and then reward them after the exercise.

You can also set up one of the mindful digital practices that we have described in this chapter. For instance, you can set up screen time monitors so you can determine if your children are using their mobile devices for several hours.

You can come up with an agreement that within the week, the child that gets the least amount of screen time will get the most number of treats come Saturday. Of course, you must live up to your promises and prepare a treat for them. The winner, of course, gets the biggest serving.

2. *Mindfulness Space and Mindfulness Huddles*

You can create some kind of safe space in your home where people can sit down, relax, and do some mindfulness meditation. Some people set up meditation rooms or meditation corners in their homes.

It doesn't have to take up a lot of space. The important thing is that it is a section of the house where you can go to be alone with your thoughts. Design it in a minimalist fashion. Keep the space clutter-free and digital technology-free.

You should put more than just one chair in the area since you're expecting the entire family to try the spot every once in a while. If you're not the chair setup kind of guy then you can layout mats of the floor, and maybe some cushions where people can sit.

Once you have your meditation corner/room set up, you can schedule certain times within the week when your entire family can gather around and practice mindfulness exercises.

These little huddles don't have to take a lot of time. You can do it once a week as an entire family and just let the meditation session last for around 10 to 20 minutes. Adjust the length of the session as needed.

Make it a rule to allow any family member to go to this designated mindfulness space. It can be your refuge from stress, problems, and confusion in your life. Allow people to join in when someone goes here to meditate. You can also use the said space for family meetings where you can discuss really important issues about your family.

3. Have Mindful Meals

Do you remember the raisin meditation exercise from earlier? You can use the same mindful practices when eating your meals. You have to skip the parts where you have to put food in your hands and stuff. Skip to the part where you chew your food well and savor the flavors in your mouth, and experience the sheer joy of good food.

But that is not all of it. Since you want to maintain your focus and mindfulness on the actual meal—meaning the food coupled with the discussion at the dinner table—you should also make it a rule that there should be no digital technology while at the table.

That means the TV should be out of sight or turned off while you have your meal. No mobile phones, tablets, or any kind of device. Everyone should focus on the meal and enjoy the few minutes when you can have an actual conversation with the people who truly matter in your life.

4. Mindfulness and Discipline

Let's face it—kids will be kids, and people will be people. Someone, sometime, somewhere will break a mindful habit. Your kid or your spouse may one day just spend too much time on their smartphone. Maybe someone in the family will binge-watch all through the night.

It happens.

Do you remember one of the phrases that we keep repeating whenever we practice mindfulness meditation? We forgive ourselves when we make mistakes. Extend the same level of forgiveness.

However, along with that mindfulness principle, as a parent, you should also impose some form of discipline on your kids just to help train them not to be too dependent on digital technology.

But how are you going to do that?

Here are a few tips:

- Listen first, ask why they binged, brought their phone to the dinner table, didn't want to join you in a mindful exercise. Don't lecture—it's the last thing they need. Learn to be understanding. In the words of Stephen Covey, "seek first to understand before you seek to be understood."

  After you have completely understood their reasons, then let them understand why you want them to participate both in your family's digital minimalism and mindfulness practices.

- Validate how they feel—acknowledge their feelings and thoughts. Empathize with them and try to see their point of view. Make sure to communicate that you understand how they feel and think.

- Redirect the dialogue to show how minimalism and mindfulness can benefit them. For example, if you discover that your child stays up late at night to play games with his or her phone, then here's what you can do.

  After listening to what they have to say, you can explain that if they don't rest early, they will have a hard time getting up in the morning, and they can be late for school the following day. Show compassion and reaffirm the fact that you care for them, and what you are doing is for their own good.

As you impose your house rules about minimalism and mindfulness, you should make it a point that you reassure your children that they can confide in you. If you have raised your voice, then apologize.

Ensure that every time you have pep talks with your kids that they feel that it is always safe to open up to you. Give them a sense of safety and reassurance that when you're leveling with them and being honest and open, they can do the same and that they can trust you.

5. Always Be Clear About the Rules

Your kids will need to know the boundaries that you have set for everyone in the house. Establishing boundaries translates to a clear definition of how far a child's autonomy goes, how much space in the house they are responsible for, and when and where they can use digital technology.

You can talk about these rules with your kids during a family meeting or a one-to-one pep talk. The important thing is that you can establish the said house rules clearly and understandably.

You can also put up reminders, like notes on the fridge and elsewhere. You can also remind your kids about these rules from time to time. You can have weekly family meetings and talk about your experiences and, of course, how everyone is doing when it comes to mindfulness and digital minimalism.

6. *Make Mornings Mindful*

Make it a rule in the house for everyone to stop using their phones and other technology for 15 minutes early in the morning. A lot of us have made it a habit to check our phones as soon as we wake up.

To help your kids practice digital minimalism and mindfulness a lot better, you can spend a mindful moment with them, as was explained earlier in this chapter. It doesn't have to take that long—just two minutes will be fine.

If they already have their phones or other devices in their hand, ask them to put them down for a minute and do a mindfulness exercise with you. All you need to do with them is this:

1. Close your eyes.
2. Breathe in and out to quiet your minds.
3. Take note and describe the emotions that you are experiencing right now.
4. Acknowledge and accept that emotion.
5. Breathe in and out, and allow these emotions to pass.

And now you can mindfully go on with your morning routine. You may need to do it with your kids from time to time until they can do it on their own.

Practicing digital mindfulness will be a big help to anyone who wants to practice digital minimalism. Minimalism allows you to separate yourself from your phones, tablets, computers, and other devices, identify the underlying emotions that influence your choices, and then purposefully and consciously use technology.

Key Takeaways

- Mindfulness as a practice has been around for hundreds of years
- Digital mindfulness is all about applying mindfulness principles and practices to our digital lives
- At any given time we can use mindfulness exercises to regain our focus and channel it into the present moment
- By using digital mindfulness, we reduce the impact and influence of digital technology in our lives

Chapter 6: More Tips and Life Hacks to Break Free of Technology Addiction

We covered technology addiction in chapter 2 of this book. A lot of the things that we talked about here, such as digital detoxes, decluttering, and minimalism, are helpful when it comes to breaking technology addiction.

In this chapter, we will go over several life hacks that you can do to break free of digital addiction.

Life Hack #1: Preventing Technology Addiction in Children

It was mentioned in an earlier chapter of this book that children are more prone to digital technology addiction. As guardians and parents, you have the responsibility to nurture and protect your children—that includes preventing digital threats.

It is easier to prevent digital technology addiction from occurring than to stop one that is already ongoing. I also understand that it is impossible to take technology out of the hands of our kids.

It is such a norm today, and they will also eventually use digital technology when they grow older. The smart way to do things is to train them early on in order to be more responsible users of digital technology.

Here are steps on how you can do that:

1. **Observe and monitor their tech usage**: You can use apps like Moment to monitor your children's use of their phones. It can give you warnings when your children have already spent too much time on their phones. We have already mentioned different screen time monitoring tools in a previous chapter as well.

2. **Watch out for the signs of tech addiction:** Review the signs and effects of tech addiction mentioned in chapter 2. If you see two or more of the side effects listed there, you should perform some direct interventions. Use the tips on

digital declutter and mindfulness mentioned in this book.

3. **Do not completely ban their internet use:** As strange as it may seem, you should never ban their internet use. Kids these days need to learn how to responsibly use digital technology. The internet is a reality of our time, and it can be a useful tool. What we need to teach is how to be more responsible when using it.

4. **Test your child's social skills—and provide some coaching if necessary:** Does your child have difficulty interacting with other kids? Not all kids have the same social skills. You may have to model and coach your child how to talk to and react to other children.

The important thing is to ensure that your child gets a lot of real-world face-to-face direct human interaction. You will also have to enforce how many hours they can use the internet and digital technology. As a parent, you need to identify your child's gifts and talents and nurture them.

Life Hack #2: What If You Can't Get Rid of Technology Completely? Tips on Minimalist Tech Use

How can you be a digital minimalist when you need technology for work or life? I agree that in our modern world, it is impossible to get rid of technology completely. Digital minimalism is not about discontinuing technology use completely.

Here are a few tips and suggestions that you can use if you need digital technology in your life:

- Don't react to social media posts. This tip is from Cal Newport's book. Don't click like, don't click the reaction buttons, don't share the post, and don't post comments. This might be challenging at first. The like button and other reaction functions on social media are quick fixes.

  If you really like what your friend posted, why not give them a call instead and tell them how you felt about it? Doing this fosters real, meaningful interactions, and allows you to use digital technology more purposefully and more mindfully.

- Consolidate all your texting time. This can also be applied to chat boxes and other work notifications. How do you do that? Let the airplane mode on your phone be the default. Schedule 30 minutes of texting time several times during your day (say 30 minutes after lunch, breakfast, and dinner so that your meals won't be interrupted).

  This will also train your coworkers, staff, clients, and other associates that your time is important, and they can't just barge into your day, hoping to get an instant response.

- Minimize computer use to work-related matters only. Make sure that you only use a computer at work. There may be times when you will need to use your computer for personal purposes—maybe to check flights, confirm orders, etc., but they should be minimal uses (maybe around five to ten minutes). The goal is to reduce computer usage outside of work. Your personal time should be used for more person-to-person interactions.

- Use your good old alarm clock. Before you watch a video on YouTube, view Facebook feeds, check Twitter tweets, or view posts on Instagram, set an alarm. You get to decide how long you want to spend on social media; however, don't set your alarm for more than one hour. After setting your alarm, go through all the social media posts that you want. When the alarm goes off, then that's it. Turn off your phone and put it in your drawer. Get back to whatever it was that you were supposed to do.

- But what if you use social media for work? Let's say that you use Facebook for social media marketing, and you need to check your ad campaign metrics. What you should do is to bookmark Facebook for Business and log into that and not your personal Facebook account. You can find the same feature in Instagram and other social media channels.

Go straight to the business section of social media and don't log on to your personal accounts. You can then check your metrics, launch new ad campaigns, and recalibrate your bot settings to better respond to product or service inquiries. Stay away from your personal Facebook account when using social media for business.

- Do a digital declutter. We already went through the details on how to do a digital declutter and inventory in chapter 3 of this book. In that chapter, we covered how to save time on your emails, how to decrease technology time, how to save time on your phone, and apps like Boomerang that will help you better manage your emails. You may want to review that chapter if you want to reduce tech time and practice digital minimalism while still using technology.

- Do a total disconnect one day each week. This is a concept that we can trace all the way to the Biblical Hebrews. It's called a Sabbath. The word is Hebrew for "day of rest." It's a day when these ancient people steer clear of all things work-related, which is something that we still do today. Stephen Covey, in his best-selling book, calls this principle *self-renewal*. You stay away from the hustle of work and digital life and spend time working on yourself.

  Designate one day each week when you will disconnect from the web and all things tech-related. Use that day to go out and get a massage, learn to cook a new recipe, sleep, clean your yard, do volunteer work for the needy, or simply just to meditate and be alone to ponder on things that are valuable to your life.

Life Hack #3: Use Art Therapy and Artistic Expression

Instead of using one of those coloring and art apps on your phone, switch to actual physical art. Let the guitar, piano, brush, clay, or mallet be your instrument and not just any art app on your phone.

One of your options when dealing with any level of digital addiction is to use art therapy [35]. It is an experiential mode of treatment where a person addresses their needs through creative expression.

Human beings are creative beings, and we have different ways of self-expression. Kids love expressing their thoughts and emotions in different ways. But we adults can also find our own way of expressing ourselves too.

That is why there are different types of art therapy/art expression, such as:

- Poetry
- Music
- Acting
- Drawing
- Dancing
- Sculpting
- Painting

Sign up for an actual class on any of these arts. If you always wanted to learn how to dance, then sign up for dance lessons. You can even sign up online. Yes, you're using digital technology, but this time you're using it purposefully and mindfully.

Life Hack #4: Use Mandalas for Meditation

Mandalas are easy to find, and you can start with them right away. They are those circular pattern designs that tend to be quite mesmerizing. Drawing and coloring mandalas can also be used as a form of meditation, which is something you can do to help you be alone with your mind and get some time for self-renewal.

I tried those and found that coloring them can be quite relaxing and meditative. Studies also show that coloring mandalas can also lead you to practice mindfulness [36].

They're cheap too, and you can find lots of patterns on Amazon or other retailers.

Here's what you should do:

1. Order a mandala book online or download mandala patterns that you can print. You can

start drawing on any piece of paper, that is, if you have some drawing skills already.

2. Set aside an hour on certain days. You can schedule your mandala time twice a week, three times a week; it's all up to you. If you're really busy, then schedule ten-minute mandala times every day.

3. Disconnect from the internet, turn off your phone, and turn off any digital tech (maybe just use your phone as a timer for this session). Set your alarm for ten minutes (or whatever time you have allotted for your mandala session).

4. Work on your mandala. Let your thoughts focus on the lines and colors that you put into your work. Take the time to appreciate the symmetry of the patterns. Pay attention to the details as much as possible.

5. When the alarm goes off, keep your mandala in a secure place. If you weren't able to complete the project today, you could always come back to it in your next session.

6. Take several deep breaths and go back to your work or the task that you had to finish that day.

Life Hack #5: Learn a New Life Skill

Choose a life skill like cooking, swimming, riding a bike, survival skills, self-defense, CPR, and first aid—anything that can be useful to you when the time comes. This is time well spent because it is your investment to become a better version of yourself.

You can sign up for a cooking class or have a friend come over to teach you a new recipe. This way, you are also enriching human experiences. You can buy a bicycle and if you don't know how to ride one then ask your neighbor or a close friend to teach you. This is something that you can't learn by just watching YouTube videos, by the way.

Life Hack #6: Pick Up a New Skill or Talent That Keeps You Away from Digital Media/Technology

This life hack is somewhat related to the previous one. Pick a skill or talent that you always wanted to learn. In my case, I always wanted to learn how to play the ukulele. So I ordered one on Amazon, and I searched for ukulele tutorials on YouTube.

I found that the chord patterns are much easier to remember since they're not that complicated compared to guitar chords. The only problem was that I bought a soprano, and it was a bit too small for my hand. But I got really good at it.

There were hundreds of tutorials on YouTube. The good part about it was that I picked a tutorial and watched YouTube for about 30 minutes until I learned the lesson very well. The great thing about it is that I was able to reduce my video streaming time.

I didn't need to watch YouTube over and over again. After I learned that lesson, I played that song or chord progression over and over for the entire day until I could do it with my eyes closed.

I really enjoyed learning new songs every day. I have also found out that you can use digital technology to help you find something that is equally enjoyable.

You can do the same. What is it that you have always wanted to try? Is it singing, drawing, boxing, dancing, pottery, jiu-jitsu, or painting? Pick something new and try your hand at it. Use tutorials that you can find on the internet.

Study one lesson per day and then disconnect from the internet so you can focus on practicing the new thing that you have learned. Keep at it until you have mastered that lesson. And then you can move on to the next one.

Life Hack #7: Use Digital Technology to Reach Out and Communicate

My team uses Zoom for meetings and presentations to clients who are overseas. However, that is not the only thing I use it for. I usually schedule virtual family reunions. Sure, we could have done that on Facebook Messenger a long time ago, but back then, my focus was just using social media and getting attention from the public.

Now, I use digital technology—Zoom, in particular—to meet up with long-lost friends and family. I don't just chat with them on Messenger, I get to see their faces and catch up. This is one of the positive ways to reinforce the proper use of digital media. I can also use it to share files and other media that might help rekindle old memories.

We're not just mindlessly using it to fill a void in our day. We use it intentionally and purposefully to reach out to our fellow human beings. Try this next time you need to use your phone. Download Zoom or Lark, Google Meet, or whatever online meeting app you would like to use.

Schedule a virtual get together with your friends—say, the following day or an hour from now—and then just go hang out with one another. Reach out and catch up to real people and not just some virtual character in a game you're playing.

Life Hack #8: Use the Power of Grey Tones

Do you know why the icons on your phone are so colorful? That is actually part of the positive psychological reinforcement to make you tap on them. That is one of the ways they were designed to attract your attention. Remember that certain colors tend to attract smartphone users.

Do you know what the least attractive colors are? It is grey scale. Studies show that when icons are in grey scale, the positive reinforcement in the design of those icons is taken away. You have removed one of the tools that steal your attention.

The good news is that grey scale color tones are already preinstalled in our devices. You can go to your phone's settings and then look for color filters. Choose grey scale as your color scheme.

Try it out and see if you feel a lot less likely to tap icons on your phone. It is the equivalent of turning off one of the pleasure switches on your device. Using your phone is no longer as fun as before because of the grey tones.

Life Hack #9: Take the Time to Read a Real Physical Book

A good friend of mine picked up a new hobby— reading actual books. It started when he saw reviews about a new TV series (yes, he's a binge-watcher) that is scheduled to premiere on Amazon called *The Wheel of Time*. It was said that this new TV series was based on a best-selling book series that spanned over two decades.

How could he have missed such a big story? He wasn't much of a book reader. But after learning about this upcoming show, he wanted to get ahead of the crowd. When *Game of Thrones* became such a big hit on TV, he loved it but never had a chance to read the actual books.

This time around, since it is rumored that *Wheel of Time* will be aired sometime in 2021, he wanted to see if he could change the experience a bit. He ordered the full 13-book set and started reading.

Some of those books were thick—and I do mean thick. Book 6 in the series had more than 600 pages in it—man, this Robert Jordan was prolific. He described his world in great detail, and the experience was so immersive.

My friend is now almost done with book 6, and I am just on the first book in the series. If you're reading a real page-turner, then you will be surprised that hours have passed since you cracked the pages open.

It's a great way to get off our screens and engage our minds. Try it. And here's a challenge that I would like you to do: read 30 pages a day. Note that with careful, focused reading, you can do that in one hour.

Life Hack #10: Go Out and See the World

You can beat technology addiction by disconnecting and going out to experience the real world.

Make a bucket list of places you want to see. Save money for weekend vacations to those places.

Going out to see the world doesn't mean your choices are only the exotic parts of the planet. Sometimes that means just getting out of the house. If you have the habit of staying stuck indoors, then spending time outdoors can already become a big improvement.

If you have a yard that desperately needs your attention, then schedule a weekend so you can work on it. Clean up your yard and get things organized.

You can even rearrange your furniture if you have no yard to fix and organize. At least you get to keep moving, and it's a great way to exercise. However, you should still dream about the places that you want to visit. Make your plans and save money for those trips.

QUICK TIP: Go out and jog for 15 to 30 minutes each day or just walk around the block. Do it every day—and I mean every day. If you meet someone, maybe a neighbor you haven't seen in awhile, spend two minutes for a short meet and greet. Savor the human interaction. It's a great way to reconnect with people and get some exercise. We also know that exercise reduces anxiety and depression, so you're also doing yourself a favor [37].

Lifehack #11: Use Minimalist Apps for Work

Going back to digital minimalism and work, there are apps that you can use at work that will help you to minimize your dependence on digital technology. We already mentioned several of these apps and plugins in the previous chapters of this book. Consider the following apps as additional resources that you can use to apply digital minimalism at work while still using tech for productivity.

Acuity

Acuity is a dynamic cloud-based appointment scheduler that integrates with many services. It even integrates with PayPal and other payment platforms, so you don't need to think about your subscription payments.

Bonsai

This is a freelancer app that you can use for managing your transactions. It integrates with a lot of other tools that you may already be using for work, from managing your invoices to timekeeping.

Gaia/Simple Habit

These apps aren't actually work apps, but you can use them during breaks. Use these apps for two to five minutes to do some guided meditation or mindfulness meditation during a busy day. It can help put some clarity on any tough, challenging day.

Squarespace

This is a tool that you can use for email campaigns, analytics, CRM, and content marketing management. It integrates into many tools, apps, and systems as well, so you don't have to jump from one system to the next. Everything you need at work will be all on one screen.

Offtime

This is an app that will block other distracting apps on your phone, like games and social media. It will even give you analytics on your phone usage so you can monitor how much time you spend on each of your installed apps.

Moment

This is a phone usage tracking app that your entire family can use. It can literally force you to stop using your phone via annoying screen alerts and other notifications.

Stay on Task

This is a productivity app on Android that is useful for someone who can get distracted easily. At certain times during the day, this app will ask you via notifications if you're still doing a task or you're doing something else. It basically reminds you to get back to work.

Lifehack #12: Life Hacks to Save Time on Office Spaces

Psychologists confirm that a cluttered environment reflects a cluttered mind. If you want to practice digital minimalism at work, then you should also practice minimalism in your office.

Here are a few tips:

- You should create as much white space as possible. That means space on your work desk that doesn't have anything on it.

Maintain a white space as big as a piece of A4-sized paper on your dominant side.

That means if you're right-handed, then this white space should be on your right-hand side of the keyboard. If you're left-handed, it should be on the left. You can use this space to sign papers, documents, reports, and organize documents. But as soon as you're doing stuff there, keep it clean and clutter-free.

- Limit the number of supplies you see on your desk. Paper clips, pens, erasers, envelopes, sticky notes, etc. shouldn't be lying around everywhere on your desk.

- Don't over-personalize your work desk. Sure, it's nice to have a picture of your cat or your family on your work desk. It serves as a motivator for you to work hard. But limit it to one or two personal items only.

- Put everything on a file. The file can be placed on the left or right of your computer screen. Use only one file, please. All papers, folders, envelopes, and work-related documents should be placed there.

- If you're using a phone in your cubicle, set it up on the dominant side of the desk. That way, you don't have to reach across to answer a call. You should also put it on the far side of the table away from your keyboard so you won't be tempted to reach out and dial now and then.

- The monitor should be at the center of your desk. It should be at eye level when you're seated on your chair and at arm's length from your body.

Chapter 7: Preventing a Relapse

It is easy for us to relapse into digital dependence, especially if we're just starting on our journey into digital minimalism. It's not going to be easy since it is very easy to open your phone and start tapping on an icon.

Here's an important mindfulness reminder: Even if you make mistakes and dip into your old habits, you can forgive yourself and bring your focus back to digital minimalism. Don't be too hard on yourself. Remember, you're not the first one to make mistakes. Pick yourself up and get back on track.

Here are a few tips that might help you prevent a relapse from happening.

1. Fill Any Empty Time Slots

As you go about trying to find new healthy habits that don't depend on digital technology, you should pay attention to your idle moments. Find something interesting that you can do to fill those idle times.

Remember that one of the lessons that have been emphasized in this book is that boredom is one of the powerful influences that make us reach for our phones and scroll through social media.

You can spend the time preparing a nice meal for you and your family, reading a book, exercising, engaging in a new hobby, or just trying to reconnect with friends. The goal is to try to stay grounded with reality and not jump back to your digital life.

2. Take Note of Your Triggers

Habits have behavioral triggers. For instance, you feel bored, and so your first instinct is to reach for your phone and to see the latest trend on Instagram. You should pay attention to these triggers and recognize them for what they are.

After that, you should try to avert the reaction to these triggers by doing something else. Here are some of the most common triggers that you should pay attention to:

- Financial insecurity
- Strained relationships
- Grief
- Depression

- Anxiety
- Feeling overwhelmed
- Fear
- Traumatic memories
- Isolation
- Loneliness
- Chronic pain
- Uncertainty

You can do mindfulness exercises to help reduce the effect of these triggers.

3. Reach Out to Someone

Whenever you can't help but use digital technology, then use it constructively. One way to do that is to reach out to someone. Check out who you can do a Skype call with. Find friends you can talk to on your messaging app. If you need professional help, then make sure there's a way for you to reach your therapist online.

4. Stay Accountable

In tip number three, the emphasis is on reaching out to get help from someone. This time, you reach out to someone to help *them*. By going out of your way—even when you're using digital tools—you still need to stay accountable for someone else.

You can use text messaging, phone calls, or video calls. The important thing is that you reach out to someone with the intent of helping them. Doing this is an acknowledgment that being alone is hard and that you are not alone in trying to overcome your dependence on digital technology.

Sometimes, when we go out of our way to help others, our own troubles seem less significant. We shift our focus away from ourselves, and in the process of reaching out to help others, we end up helping ourselves.

Key Takeaways

- As a parent or guardian, it is your responsibility to protect and nurture your children from negative influences—digital technology included.
- You can set up rules in the house when it comes to technology use.

- Learn something new, read a book, pick up a new hobby, get creative, use grey tones on your phone, and monitor your screen time.

- There are strategies that you can use to prevent a relapse, which may involve reaching out to someone for help, minding your triggers, and filling up your idle times.

Conclusion

Thank you again for purchasing this book. It is my hope that you enjoyed the content and that the information here has helped you in some way. I hope that you will practice digital minimalism and be free from technology addiction.

The next step is to use the different tips and strategies mentioned here. It takes time and practice to be a digital minimalist. I recommend that you start by doing some decluttering. That is something that you will do time and again—trust me on that one.

After that, you can try the mindfulness exercises until they become sort of a habit to you. It will take time to establish and follow digital minimalist rules in the house and at work, so be patient with yourself.

Give yourself time to reorganize and minimize things. Switching to a new minimalist approach to digital technology may be the best thing you will ever do for yourself at this time.

Thank you!

Before you go, I just wanted to say thank you for purchasing my book.

You could have picked from dozens of other books on the same topic but you took a chance and chose this one.

So, a HUGE thanks to you for getting this book and for reading all the way to the end.

Now I wanted to ask you for a small favor. ***Could you please consider posting a review on the platform? Reviews are one of the easiest ways to support the work of independent authors.***

This feedback will help me continue to write the type of books that will help you get the results you want. So if you enjoyed it, please let me know! (-:

Lastly, don't forget to grab your 2 free bonuses!

Bulletproof Confidence eBook
7 Essential Mindfulness Habits eBook

Resource Page

1 Newport, C. (2016, December 18) On Digital Minimalism.
https://www.calnewport.com/blog/2016/12/18/on-digital-minimalism/

2 Author Unknown (2020, May 25). Man creates 'cuddle curtain' to hug grandmother, video leaves netizens emotional.
https://indianexpress.com/article/trending/trending-globally/man-makes-cuddle-curtain-to-hug-grandmother-heartwarming-video-leaves-netizens-emotional-6417626/

3 Rach, J. (2020, May 15) Girl, 10, creates a 'hug curtain' using glue and a plastic shower screen so she can finally get a cuddle from her grandparents through the front door during lockdown.
https://www.dailymail.co.uk/femail/article-8319417/Lindsay-Okray-shares-touching-moment-daughter-Paige-creates-plastic-curtain-hug-grandparents.html

4 Spechler, D. (2020, May 21). I desperately miss human touch. Science may explain why.

https://www.theguardian.com/commentisfree/
2020/may/21/touch-starvation-lockdown-why

5 Cash H. et al. (2012, November 8). Internet
Addiction: A Brief Summary of Research and
Practice.
https://www.ncbi.nlm.nih.gov/pmc/articles/P
MC3480687/

5a Seyyed SA et al. (3 April 2012) Behavioral
Addiction versus Substance Addiction:
Correspondence of Psychiatric and
Psychological Views
https://www.ncbi.nlm.nih.gov/pmc/articles/P
MC3354400/

5b Grant JE et al. (1 September 2011)
Introduction to Behavioral Addictions.
https://www.ncbi.nlm.nih.gov/pmc/articles/P
MC3164585/

5c Potenza M. N. (2008). Review. The
neurobiology of pathological gambling and drug
addiction: an overview and new findings.
Philosophical transactions of the Royal Society
of London. Series B, Biological Sciences,
363(1507), 3181–3189.
https://doi.org/10.1098/rstb.2008.0100

6 Kuss D.J., Lopez-Fernandez O. (2016 March 22). Internet addiction and problematic Internet use: A systematic review of clinical research.
https://www.ncbi.nlm.nih.gov/pmc/articles/PMC4804263/

6a Aguilera-Manrique, G., Márquez-Hernández, V. V., Alcaraz-Córdoba, T., Granados-Gámez, G., Gutiérrez-Puertas, V., & Gutiérrez-Puertas, L. (2018). The relationship between nomophobia and the distraction associated with smartphone use among nursing students in their clinical practicum. PloS one, 13(8), e0202953.
https://doi.org/10.1371/journal.pone.0202953

7 Karisson J. et al. (2019 September 24). Associations between Problematic Gambling, Gaming, and Internet Use: A Cross-Sectional Population Survey.
https://europepmc.org/article/PMC/6778943

8 Makalesi A, Macit HB (2019 June). A Research On Social Media Addiction and Dopamine Driven Feedback.
https://www.researchgate.net/publication/333

774040_A_Research_On_Social_Media_Addic
tion_and_Dopamine_Driven_Feedback

9 Haynes, Trevor (2018, May 1). Dopamine, Smartphones & You: A battle for your time. http://sitn.hms.harvard.edu/flash/2018/dopa mine-smartphones-battle-time/

10 Author unknown (2020) Computer/Internet Addiction Symptoms, Causes and Effects. https://www.psychguides.com/behavioral-disorders/computer-internet-addiction/

11 Willard, Stephen (2013, February 12) Study: People Check Their Cell Phones Every Six Minutes, 150 Times A Day. https://www.elitedaily.com/news/world/study-people-check-cell-phones-minutes-150-times-day

12 Ward AF, et al. (2017 April 3) Brain Drain: The Mere Presence of One's Own Smartphone Reduces Available Cognitive Capacity. http://www.journals.uchicago.edu/doi/10.1086 /691462

13 Gallagher, B. (2017, September 21). Modern Media Is a DoS Attack on Your Free Will.

http://nautil.us/issue/52/the-hive/modern-media-is-a-dos-attack-on-your-free-will

14 Lewis, P. (2017 October 6) Our minds can be hijacked': the tech insiders who fear a smartphone dystopia.
https://www.theguardian.com/technology/2017/oct/05/smartphone-addiction-silicon-valley-dystopia

15 Fischer S., McCabe D. (2018 February 6). Kids are flooding the internet.
https://www.axios.com/kids-are-flooding-the-internet-youtube-facebook-video-6d97a4d7-93cb-43eb-8fa1-150ed25a7612.html

16 Kamenetz, A. (2017 October 19). Young Children Are Spending Much More Time In Front Of Small Screens.
https://www.npr.org/sections/ed/2017/10/19/558178851/young-children-are-spending-much-more-time-in-front-of-small-screens

16a Stockdale L. et al. (4 October 2017) Cool, callous and in control: superior inhibitory control in frequent players of video games with violent content.
https://esource.dbs.ie/handle/10788/1063

17 Kats, R. (2017 November 16). Obsessed Much? Mobile Addiction Is Real. https://www.emarketer.com/Article/Obsessed-Much-Mobile-Addiction-Real/1016759

18 Ibid.

19 Twenge, J. M. (2017 September) Have Smartphones Destroyed a Generation?. https://www.theatlantic.com/magazine/archive/2017/09/has-the-smartphone-destroyed-a-generation/534198/

19a Dave Mosher (17 July 2011) High Wired: Does Addictive Internet Use Restructure the Brain? https://www.scientificamerican.com/article/does-addictive-internet-use-restructure-brain/

19b Lin F, Yan Z, Yasong D, Lindi Q, et al.: Abnormal white matter integrity in adolescents with internet addiction disorder: A tract based spatial statistics study. PLoS One 2012; 7:e30253.

19c Weng CB, Qian RB, Xian-Ming F, Bin L, et al.: Gray matter and white matter abnormalities in on line game addictions. Eur J Radiol 2013; 82: 1308–1312

19d Hou H, Jia S, Hu S, Fan R, et al.: Reduced striatal dopamine transporters in people with internet addiction disorders. J Biomed Biotechnol 2012; 2012: 1–5. DOI: 10.1155/2012/854524.

20 Neport C. (2019 February 5) Digital Minimalism: Choosing a Focused Life in a Noisy World. https://www.amazon.com/Digital-Minimalism-Choosing-Focused-Noisy/dp/0525536515

21 Nam T. (2013 November 17) Technology Use and Work-Life Balance. https://psycnet.apa.org/doi/10.1007/s11482-013-9283-1

22 George M., et al. (2017 May 3) Concurrent and Subsequent Associations Between Daily Digital Technology Use and High-Risk Adolescents' Mental Health Symptoms. https://doi.org/10.1111/cdev.12819

23 Melissa G. Hunt, Rachel Marx, Courtney Lipson, and Jordyn Young (2018). No More FOMO: Limiting Social Media Decreases Loneliness and Depression. Journal of Social

and Clinical Psychology: Vol. 37, No. 10, pp. 751-768.

https://doi.org/10.1521/jscp.2018.37.10.751

24 Fuller C, Lehman E, Hicks S. (2017 October 27). Bedtime Use of Technology and Associated Sleep Problems in Children. https://dx.doi.org/10.1177%2F2333794X17736972

25 Bhat S., et al. (2018 April) "To sleep, perchance to tweet": in-bed electronic social media use and its associations with insomnia, daytime sleepiness, mood, and sleep duration in adults. https://doi.org/10.1016/j.sleh.2017.12.004

26 Sara Thomee, Annika Harenstam, Mats Hagberg (2011 January 31) Mobile phone use and stress, sleep disturbances, and symptoms of depression among young adults - a prospective cohort study. https://doi.org/10.1186/1471-2458-11-66

27 Misra S., et al. (2014 July 1) The iPhone Effect: The Quality of In-Person Social Interactions in the Presence of Mobile Devices.

https://journals.sagepub.com/doi/10.1177/001
39169514539755

27a Elizabeth Segran (30 July 2015) What
Really Happens to Your Brain and Body During
a Digital Detox.
https://www.fastcompany.com/3049138/what-
really-happens-to-your-brain-and-body-during-
a-digital-detox

27b Tosini, G., Ferguson, I., & Tsubota, K.
(2016). Effects of blue light on the circadian
system and eye physiology. Molecular Vision,
22, 61–72.

27c Naciye Guliz Ugura, Tugba Koca (2015)
Time for Digital Detox: Misuse of Mobile
Technology and Phubbing.
https://pdf.sciencedirectassets.com/277811/1-
s2.0-S1877042815X00334/1-s2.0-
S1877042815039701/main.pdf

27d van Velthoven, M. H., Powell, J., & Powell,
G. (2018). Problematic smartphone use: Digital
approaches to an emerging public health
problem. Digital health, 4, 2055207618759167.
https://doi.org/10.1177/2055207618759167

27e Fernandez, D. P., Kuss, D. J., & Griffiths, M. D. (2020). Short-term abstinence effects across potential behavioral addictions: A systematic review. Clinical psychology review, 76, 101828. https://doi.org/10.1016/j.cpr.2020.101828

27f Annalise G. Mabe, K. Jean Forney, Pamela K. Keel (24 January 2014) Do you "like" my photo? Facebook use maintains eating disorder risk. https://onlinelibrary.wiley.com/doi/abs/10.100 2/eat.22254

28 Sue McGreevey (2011 January 21) Eight weeks to a better brain: Meditation study shows changes associated with awareness, stress. http://news.harvard.edu/gazette/story/2011/01 /eight-weeks-to-a-better-brain/

29 Jon Hamilton (2008 October 2) Think You're Multitasking? Think Again. https://www.npr.org/templates/story/story.ph p?storyId=95256794

30 James Carmody, Ruth A. Baer (2007 September 25) Relationships Between Mindfulness Practice and Levels of Mindfulness, Medical and Psychological

Symptoms and Well-Being in a Mindfulness-Based Stress Reduction Program.
http://www.ncbi.nlm.nih.gov/pubmed/178993
51

31 Joanna J Arch, Michelle G Craske (2006 February 7). Mechanisms of Mindfulness: Emotion Regulation Following a Focused Breathing Induction.
http://www.ncbi.nlm.nih.gov/pubmed/164606
68

32 Grossman P., et al. (2004 July) Mindfulness-based Stress Reduction and Health Benefits. A Meta-Analysis.
http://www.ncbi.nlm.nih.gov/pubmed/152562
93

33 Emma M. Seppala (2014 May 28) A Gift Of Loving Kindness Meditation.
http://www.emmaseppala.com/gift-loving-kindness-meditation/

34 Chris Tachibana (2013 February 1) Five steps to a successful sabbatical.
http://www.sciencemag.org/features/2013/02/
five-steps-successful-sabbatical

35 Author Unknown (2019 July 26) Using Art Therapy to Treat Addiction.
https://www.oxfordtreatment.com/addiction-treatment/experiential-therapy/art/

36 Michail Mantzios, Kyriaki Giannou (2018 January 30) When Did Coloring Books Become Mindful? Exploring the Effectiveness of a Novel Method of Mindfulness-Guided Instructions for Coloring Books to Increase Mindfulness and Decrease Anxiety.
https://www.ncbi.nlm.nih.gov/pmc/articles/PMC5797627/

37 Anderson, E., & Shivakumar, G. (2013). Effects of exercise and physical activity on anxiety. Frontiers in psychiatry, 4, 27.
https://doi.org/10.3389/fpsyt.2013.00027